'This book offers an engaging and insightful deep dive into the challenges and opportunities facing nation brands in Europe. Practitioners of place marketing, tourism, international relations and diplomacy can gain a broad understanding of the geo-political, cultural and economic factors that coalesce around a place brand, and scholars and students alike will benefit from the thorough cross-section of cases featured. In light of changing current events, this book is needed now more than ever.'

Dr Giannina Warren, *Senior Lecturer,*
Middlesex University, UK

Nation Branding in Europe

This book provides an explanation of nation branding theory and practice within the European context, exploring how countries build and manage their reputations globally.

Each chapter focuses on a specific European country, selected from a cross section of large, medium-sized and small countries to provide a breadth of cases from across the continent. The chapters are written from a wide range of academic and practitioner perspectives.

Nation Branding in Europe is valuable supplementary reading for advanced undergraduate, postgraduate and doctoral students interested in nation branding and will appeal to students from marketing, communications and international relations disciplines. Outside of academia, the book will be of interest to those working in the areas of public diplomacy and strategic communications, as well as public relations and branding practitioners involved in designing nation branding campaigns.

João Freire is Professor at Ipam/Universidade Europeia, Portugal, and a researcher at ICNOVA in Lisbon, Portugal.

Routledge Focus on Nation Branding
Series Editor: Keith Dinnie

This series of short-form books approaches the fast-growing subject of Nation Branding, in which the principles of brand strategy and management are applied to countries, from both a geographical and thematic perspective. It is designed to provide a critical analysis of the ways in which specific countries throughout the world build and develop their brands; in their totality, the books will provide a complete picture of the theories, concepts and practices of Nation Branding globally.

Nation Branding in Europe
Edited by João Freire

For more information about this series, please visit www.routledge.com/Routledge-Focus-on-Nation-Branding/book-series/RFNB

Nation Branding in Europe

Edited by João Freire

Routledge
Taylor & Francis Group

LONDON AND NEW YORK

First published 2022
by Routledge
2 Park Square, Milton Park, Abingdon, Oxon OX14 4RN

and by Routledge
605 Third Avenue, New York, NY 10158

Routledge is an imprint of the Taylor & Francis Group, an informa business

British Library Cataloguing-in-Publication Data
A catalogue record for this book is available from the British Library

Library of Congress Cataloging-in-Publication Data
Names: Freire, João (Editor) editor.
Title: Nation branding in Europe / edited by João Freire.
Description: New York, NY : Routledge, 2022. |
    Series: Routledge focus on nation branding | Includes
    bibliographical references and index.
Identifiers: LCCN 2021020434 (print) | LCCN 2021020435
    (ebook)
Subjects: LCSH: Place marketing—Europe—Case studies. |
    Branding (Marketing)—Europe—Case studies. | Nation-state. |
    International relations.
Classification: LCC HF5415.12.E8 N38 2022 (print) | LCC
    HF5415.12.E8 (ebook) | DDC 914.0068/8—dc23
LC record available at https://lccn.loc.gov/2021020434
LC ebook record available at https://lccn.loc.gov/2021020435

ISBN: 978-0-367-54013-5 (hbk)
ISBN: 978-0-367-54014-2 (pbk)
ISBN: 978-1-003-08405-1 (ebk)

DOI: 10.4324/9781003084051

Typeset in Times New Roman
by Apex CoVantage, LLC

Contents

Contributors

Christophe Alaux Tenure-track Professor, Dean of the French Public Management & Territorial Governance Institute (IMPGT) at Aix-Marseille University, he is also Director of the French Chair 'New Place Marketing and Attractiveness,' which is funded by 30 French local authorities and companies.

ORCID: https://orcid.org/0000-0003-4165-9824.

Malcolm Allan Malcolm Allan is the President of Bloom Consulting, which specializes in country, city and urban brand strategy. He has worked as a place brand strategist for 20 years on a variety of projects for countries and cities around the world for Placebrands, Locum Consulting, Colliers International and Placematters. Prior to doing so, his career was in urban planning, economic development and inward investment, working for the United Kingdom and major city governments. He has contributed articles on place brand practice to City Nation Place and The Place Brand Observer and is currently exploring the contribution of place brand strategy to climate change mitigation.

Marcus Andersson Marcus Andersson is the founder of Future Place Leadership, a Nordic consultancy focusing on the development, innovation and marketing of places. He has published a range of books, handbooks, articles and reports on topics such as place branding, talent attraction for places, investment promotion, place leadership and placemaking.

ORCID: https://orcid.org/0000-0002-7544-0436.

Simon Anholt Simon Anholt coined the term 'nation brand' and is the world's leading expert on national image. He has written six books and advised the governments, Presidents and Prime Ministers of 56 nations. He founded the Nation Brands and City Brands Indexes in 2005 and the Good Country Index in 2014.

ORCID: https://orcid.org/0000-0002-3382-6605.

Magdalena Florek Dr hab. Magdalena Florek is an Associate Professor at Poznan University of Economics and Business, Poland. Co-founder and board member of the International Place Branding Association. Co-founder and board member of The European Place Marketing Institute BEST PLACE. Senior Fellow at the Institute of Place Management. Consultant and co-author of numerous place branding strategies in Poland.

ORCID: https://orcid.org/0000-0003-3088-2027.

João Freire Dr. João R. Freire is a professor at Ipam/Universidade Europeia and a researcher at ICNOVA in Lisbon, Portugal. João's background in economics initially led him to work in the fields of finance and marketing for several multinational companies in Brazil, Portugal and the United Kingdom. His main interest is in branding and, more specifically, place branding. João is an author, consultant and frequent speaker on branding topics.

ORCID: https://orcid.org/0000-0003-1199-412X.

Jarosław Górski Dr Jarosław Górski is Assistant Professor at University of Warsaw, Faculty of Economic Sciences. Co-founder of International Place Branding Association. Co-founder and board member of The European Place Marketing Institute BEST PLACE. Place marketing advisor in the Association of Polish Cities. Consultant in many marketing projects for cities, regions, public and private entities.

ORCID: https://orcid.org/0000-0002-5783-1038

Robert Govers Robert Govers is the author of the award-winning book *Imaginative Communities* (2018). He is founding chairman of the International Place Branding Association, co-editor of the quarterly journal, *Place Branding and Public Diplomacy* and a contributor to Apolitical, the World Economic Forum Agenda and the Economist Intelligence Unit Perspectives.

ORCID: https://orcid.org/0000-0001-6312-9029.

Mark Henry Mark Henry is the Central Marketing Director of Tourism Ireland, the organization that promotes overseas tourism to the island of Ireland. He has 20 years' experience in destination promotion and previously worked in the market research and e-business sectors. Mark possesses both MA (Psychology) and MBA degrees from University College Dublin.

ORCID: https://orcid.org/0000-0002-1418-7668.

Cecilia Pasquinelli Cecilia Pasquinelli, PhD, is Assistant Professor of Business Management at the University of Naples Parthenope. Previously, she worked as a researcher at the Gran Sasso Science Institute, Italy and at the University of Uppsala, Sweden. Her research has focused on place branding, place marketing, urban tourism, tourism management and local and regional development.

ORCID: https://orcid.org/0000-0002-4924-9398.

Kirill Rozhkov Kirill Rozhkov is Professor at the Higher School of Business in the HSE University (Moscow, Russia). He is also a Senior Fellow of the Institute of Place Management (Manchester, UK). His research interests lie in place marketing, place management and place branding.

ORCID: https://orcid.org/0000-0003-1765-1611

Anna Schwan Dr Anna Schwan holds a PhD degree in Communication Studies, specializing in place branding and public diplomacy. She has been researching and working in the area for more than 15 years, being one of the forerunners in this field in Germany. Anna lectures at the University of Hamburg and runs the agency Schwan Communications that has established several place branding campaigns for Germany, Berlin and Hamburg.

Gildo Seisdedos As a professor at IE Business School, Gildo Seisdedos combines teaching, research and consulting activities in the fields of urban planning, local policies and city marketing. He has prepared studies on urban planning and design at London School of Economics (LSE) and University of California, Los Angeles (UCLA). He has served as the director of IE's marketing programmes for 8 years and is passionate about teaching.

ORCID: https://orcid.org/0000-0002-6753-4360

José Filipe Torres Jose Filipe Torres advises place leaders such as heads of state, directors of national tourism organizations and investment promotion agencies on strategy and branding. Beyond Mr Torres' work across five continents, he has collaborated directly with the Organisation for Economic Co-operation and Development (OECD) and the World Economic Forum (WEF). Mr Torres has been a guest speaker at universities including Harvard and the London Business School. His publications include the Bloom Consulting Country Ranking, his latest book, *Nation Brand Builders* and the Digital Country Index derived from Bloom Consulting's analytical software, Digital Demand (D2©).

Foreword by the Series Editor

The cases in this book vividly illustrate the rich diversity of approaches to nation branding taken by different European countries. This reflects the varied institutional landscapes to be found across Europe. The book's chapters are written by a range of academic and practitioner experts, each of whom brings a unique sensibility to bear upon the country in question and that country's nation branding activities. Some contributors are complementary about the nation branding efforts of the country they are covering whilst other contributors are more critical. It is, of course, up to the reader to reach their own conclusions regarding the quality of nation branding performance of each country.

Expertly edited by João Ricardo Freire, this volume is intended to be of interest to both academic and practitioner audiences. It is the first book in the *Routledge Focus on Nation Branding* series. Forthcoming volumes in the series will cover nation branding in other regions of the world, taking the same eclectic and thought-provoking approach as this book on nation branding in Europe.

Keith Dinnie
Series Editor, *Routledge Focus on Nation Branding*

1 Introduction

João Freire

The various editions of *Nation Branding: Concepts, Issues, Practice* by Keith Dinnie highlight nation branding cases from various continents. This supplemental book, *Nation Branding in Europe*, is based on specific cases of nation branding strategies in Europe. Academics and practitioners from various European countries were invited to participate and write a chapter on the branding of a specific European country. The chapters are based on the knowledge and opinions of these various experts.

Given that Europe is composed of over 40 countries, we were unable to include one case for each country. We decided the best approach would be to include cases from a few countries that would represent what is currently being done in Europe.

Twelve European countries were selected for this edition. Our criteria for selecting the countries were size and diversity. To meet the size requirement the six largest countries in Europe – France, Germany, Italy, Russia, Spain and the United Kingdom – were selected. To meet the diversity requirement, three medium-sized and three small-sized countries from different European regions were selected. The medium-sized countries include the Netherlands (representative of Northern Europe), Poland (representative of Eastern Europe) and Sweden (representative of Scandinavia). The three small-size countries include Ireland due to its success as a country for foreign direct investment (FDI); Portugal due to its success as a tourism destination and Estonia due to its economic boom and for being known as one of the three Baltic tigers.

The goal of this book is to understand how various European countries are developing their nation brand strategy. Do countries have a nation-branding strategy? Who manages the nation brand? Is there a governance model to help the brand management process? What are the challenges related to the management and implementation of a nation brand strategy?

DOI: 10.4324/9781003084051-1

By and large, it is apparent that all governments are committed to promoting their country in international markets. Nonetheless each country approaches nation branding distinctly. These cases also highlight the complexity of a place brand strategy. Only a few countries have been able to manage their brand strategically and consistently over the long term.

From these cases, we can conclude that just a few countries have developed a cohesive successful branding strategy. These countries understand what they are doing and have clearly put into practice a long-term nation brand strategy. These nation brand strategies are research-based, include a well-defined governance model and take a multisectoral approach. Those nation brand strategies typically involve the central government, but not necessarily a particular political party. Various stakeholders of society are involved. In doing so, the nation brand strategy is not linked to a political party and is easily accepted by various governments. This is key for maintaining a long-term brand strategy. One can evaluate how successful those strategies have been through the continued growth of the economies of these countries.

However, there are some countries that regard nation branding as a political tool. When this happens the nation brand strategy suffers from limitations of scope, duration, involvement and effectiveness. The strategy is developed by the particular political party in power and is based solely on its vision for the country. In these cases, a model of governance may exist but the strategy is grounded in the political vision and opinions of the current government in power. The strategy is not research-based. This also means that the strategy will change depending on the political party in power and that some politicians might be willing to change course if they think they will win votes. When this happens, the independence of the brand managers is also reduced.

A less effective approach to nation branding is where countries develop a number of advertising campaigns that they consider to be a nation-branding strategy. With this approach, the stakeholder engagement is generally low, the governance model is unclear and the market is poorly understood.

Some countries take a sector-by-sector approach to the country's branding strategy. When this occurs it often means that the more powerful and better organized industries take over the brand. This is most evident in the tourism industry, which operates in a highly competitive marketplace. The problem with this approach is that many sectors get left out of the nation brand strategy. We can even say that in these countries no nation brand strategy exists; what actually exists is a destination brand strategy.

We can conclude from these cases that one of the biggest challenges in running a country as a brand is the strategic management of different places within a country, whether they are cities or regions. Cities and regions have elected governments that often have their own branding strategies. In some cases, there is very little communication between the cities, regions and the central government. Lack of communication between these places can result in an inconsistent message, which puts the implementation of a more effective overarching strategy for the country at risk. This is most commonly seen in the cases of larger countries that typically have strong cities and regions.

There are three important concepts that emerge from the case studies: brand architecture, governance models and research-based strategy. An effective brand architecture system enables places within the country to communicate with a central government. Therefore, a well-defined brand architecture makes it possible to manage the country's brand more efficiently. Developing a model of governance that involves a wide range of stakeholders is key since doing this gives the brand a better chance of resisting changes in government and increases its efficiency over the long term. Finally, a nation brand strategy should be developed on the basis of research. A research-based strategy facilitates two things: acceptance of the strategy and the involvement of a wide range of stakeholders.

Each contributor in this book was selected on the basis of their knowledge of the country and their expertise in the field of place branding. The contributors have distinct backgrounds and their current positions are varied as well. Some are academics who research place branding, some are consultants and some work for organizations that manage a place brand. Each chapter is written by a different expert therefore, in addition to bringing their professional expertise on the subject, each contributor lends their own personality and style to the chapter. One interesting note is that despite the contributor's varied backgrounds and current positions, they all approach nation branding in a broadly similar way.

After reading this book, our hope is that readers will understand the concept of nation branding better and appreciate the strategies that different European countries have implemented.

2 Germany

Anna Schwan

Communicating Germany: how the quest for an innovative image is shaping Germany's current place branding activities

Public diplomacy and nation branding have become an important instrument of power in the media societies of today. Bundling the multitude of stakeholders of a country, finding clear messages to portray that place and placing these messages with the media in order to reach the right target groups has become a key attribute of a nation's foreign relations efforts.

Ever since the American political scientist Joseph Nye coined the term 'soft power' in the journal *Foreign Policy* in 1990, it has become an important concept in the theory of international relations (Nye, 2005). Referring to the image cultivation of countries, Nye stated that the creation and maintenance of a positive image increases its attractiveness to investors, professionals and the general public. He distinguished the term from 'hard power,' that is, military and economic power. However, today it is undisputed that soft power also forms the basis for security policy and economic strength. The importance of Nye's concept cannot be underestimated in meeting the challenges of the 21st century. A country's reputation is closely linked with soft power. But it does not come of itself. It is a matter of political will and communication strategy.

Today, political parties are organized as political brands, ministries actively put their messages on the agenda of the domestic media – and the state tries to present itself positively abroad, using PR and marketing methods in various place branding and public diplomacy campaigns.

Anyone who applies the theories of PR research, political communication and brand management to modern governmental communication abroad will recognize clear overlaps: political communication can be understood as integrated communication. Its goals are image enhancement, credibility enhancement and, above all, confidence-building. PR and marketing

DOI: 10.4324/9781003084051-2

thus become fundamental components of political work. As a result, brand management has also successfully penetrated the political arena. Identity-oriented theories of brand management play a special role here (Bennett, 1998; Bergler, 2008): Brands are created through the dynamic interplay of image and identity. Identity, however, concerns both the creation of an own identity and its communication to the target groups.

Strategic Communication Abroad

With increasing research on political communications in recent years, a variety of definitions of different theories from marketing, PR, place branding, public diplomacy and soft power has emerged. In order to combine the findings and apply them to the entirety of political communication abroad, it may be useful to establish a new key phrase. This counts especially for Germany with its federal state system and its federal external communication. This is why the concept of 'Strategic Communication Abroad' was created (Schwan, 2010). It defines a long-term, strategically oriented communication in specific target countries that integrates various actors and acts in a persuasive manner to build confidence in the nation communicating. At both actor and recipient level, Strategic Communication Abroad involves state and non-state actors. Probably the most important factor for rewarding communication is the joined-up creation and careful coordination of the image portrayed, both domestically and abroad. Today's interconnected digital media demands coherent communications towards audiences inside the country and abroad. The aim of all Strategic Communication Abroad is to improve the image of the nation internationally, but the overriding concern is to expand the state's scope of power in international relations – in other words, to provide soft power. Translating the goals of Strategic Communication Abroad into everyday practice is a complex project. The duration, form of address and intended effect determine in equal measure how, through which channels, when, why and over what period of time communication is carried out. Addressing large audiences is possible above all through asymmetrical, that is, one-sided, communication of the mass media and large advertising campaigns: this is how attention is generated in the short term. Based on this, symmetrical, that is, dialogue-oriented communication can build up lasting trust and long-term relationships. The interaction between these levels secures visibility and efficiency in communications.

Within this framework, several campaigns promoting Germany as a country of innovation are presented here. As a federal country, Germany has special challenges when it comes to place branding: all campaigns depend on involving the federal states. A large proportion of place branding campaigns are initiated by the federal states themselves with no coordination with the Federal Government. The Federal Ministries and the Federal Government may contribute guidelines and umbrella campaigns, but depend on the states to contribute. An exemption is the foreign cultural and educational policy, which has been considered the 'third pillar' of foreign policy in Germany since the late 1960s and is executed by the Foreign Ministry and the Goethe-Institut. In all other place branding communications, whether tourism- or business-oriented, the states have their own communication strategies.

Foreign cultural policy and the Goethe-Institut

Foreign cultural policy was named an axiom of foreign policy in the 1960s by the then Federal Chancellor Willy Brandt. It played an important role in the reconciliation with Eastern Europe. Foreign cultural policy has retained its status to this day and cultural outreach plays a special role within Germany's strategic communication abroad (see: Olaf Zimmermann/Theo Geißler: Die dritte Säule: Auswärtige Kultur- und Bildungspolitik, 2018). The Goethe-Institut is the organization that draws up strategies and implements a wide range of concepts, acting in a manner similar to the British Council or the Institut Français. With its projects, the Goethe-Institut aims to convey a diversified, modern image of Germany. Its many different projects present a country open to the world, rooted in the values of the European Enlightenment, and engaged in dialogue with other cultures. The projects are implemented on eye level with the target groups, thus the focus here lies on dialogue-based communication within the network, primarily aimed at artistic talents and elites as well as opinion leaders in the cultural area. Dialogue-based communication implies symmetrical communication and long-term outcomes. The aim is to establish relationships and new communities while projecting a positive image of Germany. The projects include journalist tours to Germany, scholarships for artists, artist-in-residence programmes and support for artist trips and world tours. Large international advertising campaigns are rare; the Goethe-Institut targets smaller cultural groups rather than large audiences.

The concept of culture on which the work of the Goethe-Institut is based goes far beyond classical definitions of culture. It encompasses areas such as religion, technology and education and can therefore reflect very different themes. From a purely communicative point of view, this concept is facing a dilemma: how to combine the cultural diversity that is to be depicted and communicated with a high degree of recognition of 'Brand Germany'? Cultural communication serves the realization of foreign policy goals. However, it must be free in its content definition and it must promote diversified projects to maintain its credibility and to create impact. But this may lead to a lack of consistency in the messages sent out in cultural communications. This is where framework guidelines, which the Goethe-Institut has agreed upon with the German Foreign Office, are intended to help. These include the obligation to promote the general objectives of German foreign policy and the Federal Government's commitment to the diversity and independence of the cultural organizations.

Communicating Germany as an innovative business location

Germany is one of the most important business locations worldwide, even though this status is currently being challenged by the digital transformation and globalized economy. This applies both to traditional economic sectors such as the automotive industry (think of Tesla and disruptive car manufacturers in the field of electromobility) and to future industries such as IT, renewable energies or life sciences. It is not only in Germany itself that a growing number of voices are raised about whether the digital transformation could be missed by German SMEs. Germany's economy is seen in the 'innovators' dilemma,' missing out on potential for disruption (Christensen, 1997). In the study 'Germany in the eyes of the world,' as a business location Germany is still rated as excellent, but many contributors wonder 'whether Germany is not losing touch in times of digitization. There is a great deal of catching up to do in terms of the willingness to try out new things and also to accept failure' (Germany in the eyes of the world, 2018). These concerns are raised despite the fact that in the same year Germany was named 'Most competitive economy in the world' by the World Economic Forum (The Global Competitiveness Report, 2018). Accordingly, it is important to pay special attention to the innovative image of the business location and to market 'Made in Germany' innovation successes internationally.

To this end, the Federal Ministry for Economic Affairs and Energy has launched several umbrella initiatives, for example 'Germany works,' the general campaign for Germany as a business location, and 'German Accelerator,' a B2B initiative that brings German start-ups to the United States and Asia and networks them with investors and companies abroad. 'Germany works' closely collaborates with the business development agencies of the German states and organizes joint trade fair appearances and high-profile events, as well as traditional advertising in leading international media. The 'German Accelerator,' on the other hand, focuses on bringing the innovative power of German start-ups to the world and tells the stories of these business entrepreneurs in specific target markets. With offices in Silicon Valley, New York, Boston and Singapore, it sets clear priorities in the world's innovation regions. Start-up pitches, networking events and coaching sessions with partners from the region take place on a weekly basis, and all of them are advertised and distributed via digital (social) media channels. Thus, the 'German Accelerator' aims not only to support startups from Germany but also to facilitate their success stories and tell these stories to the right B2B target groups.

The future Hamburg award: a case study from Germany's economic hub

The topic of innovation in place branding is also of particular importance for the city of Hamburg. As the second largest city in Germany with almost 2 million inhabitants, as a federal state in itself and as one of the economic hubs in Germany, the city seeks to attract more foreign investors, especially from future-oriented industries. Google, Facebook, Airbus and COSCO have already opened up their European subsidiaries here, but development is currently stagnating – Tesla is building its gigafactory in Brandenburg, Microsoft has favoured Munich as its home base and Berlin is well ahead in terms of start-ups.

Hamburg is, like all federal states, rather independent in its political marketing decisions and FDI campaigns. The city has developed a strong brand within Germany, but is not known too well outside the neighbouring countries and Scandinavia. Especially outside the European Union, Hamburg has hardly any connotations, unlike Berlin or Munich. The organizations 'Hamburg Marketing' and 'Hamburg Invest' are set to change this and have developed international campaigns over recent years to make Hamburg more visible on a global scale and to attract more foreign business. The 'Future Hamburg' campaign is the latest addition to the campaigns of the city. It presents Hamburg's economic clusters – aviation, logistics, maritime technologies, renewable energies, life sciences and creative industries – and markets them in the city's target countries: Scandinavia, the United Kingdom, the United States, China and the Middle East are particularly in focus. On-site B2B events as part of the 'Hamburg On Tour' programmes, which present Hamburg as a liveable, vibrant and sustainable location in capitals around the world, are just as much a part of the campaign as success stories of Hamburg-based founders and companies.

However, the heart of the campaign is the 'Future Hamburg Award,' an international start-up competition. It was created in 2018 to bring international start-ups – especially from industries such as aviation, maritime, renewable energies, mobility, life sciences – to Hamburg to build solutions for the city of the future in collaboration with urban investors and companies. Thus, Hamburg intends to establish itself as a laboratory for best practices and model solutions. Innovative ideas are to be developed here and made scalable for the German and European market. The award thus pursues two goals: to attract attention and create visibility for Hamburg as a location for innovation among entrepreneurs and founders from future-oriented industries and to attract interesting start-ups with established business models to the city. Another target for the initiators, Hamburg Marketing and Hamburg Invest, is to emerge from the shadow of Berlin as a German start-up hot spot and the city with the coolest image in the country. In addition, a third aim is to highlight Hamburg's economic strength in other sectors than the traditional port and to put the city on the international map.

In the first year of the campaign, almost 200 startups took part in the award and the attention for Hamburg as a start-up location was significantly increased: a media reach of 962 million, a social media reach of 768,000, social event reach of 147,000, as well as approximately 4,000 guests at real life events such as the Kick Off in London and the award ceremony at the Online Marketing Rockstars in Hamburg, one of the largest online marketing conferences in Europe, speak for themselves. Accordingly, the award will be continued in future years.

As interesting as the successes of this city branding campaign may be, they do reveal a problem of German place branding: the campaign has not been coordinated in any way with the initiatives of the federal government or the other states. Established international resources were neither used nor was the campaign aligned with similar programmes by Federal agencies. Instead, the Future Hamburg Award relied exclusively on its own local and international partners. In this way, not only has international reach been lost but also a lot of potential within Germany.

Germany is perceived well internationally, even though a strategic communication approach is missing

This is typical for the communicative challenges of the federal structure of Germany. And it may be a reason for another interesting result of the cited study on the image of Germany: the country is perceived as weak in its marketing (Germany in the eyes of the world, 2018). The findings state:

> Germany is perceived as being weak in terms of nation branding. Why does it not market itself more vigorously and in a more varied light? Efforts to raise Germany's cultural profile have clearly proven inadequate despite all the evidence of considerable outside interest. Our interviewees question why Germany does not invest more extensively in cultural marketing as a strategic tool, a practice long since adopted by other nations.
>
> (Germany in the eyes of the world, 2018, p. 4)

This may come as a surprise, since 'Made in Germany' is a strong brand and the country of origin–effect of German products, especially in car manufacturing and machinery, is very positive. Also, in recent nation brand indices, Germany is among the most popular countries in the world (Anholt-Ipsos Nation Brands Index (NBI), 2019). However, when it comes to strategic marketing and international communications, the federal government and the states, as well as adjacent agencies such as the Chamber of Commerce abroad, are seen as underperforming. The country's place branding falls short of international expectations and, as a result, may fall short in its soft power.

Especially in a world that is constantly changing and facing great challenges in the coming years, open, truthful and good communication can decrease uncertainties, steer positive action and create international communities. This requires modern, forward-looking Strategic Communication Abroad, that is 'state of the art' in terms of communication and bundles the innovative strength of the country and its regions. To achieve this, cooperation between the federal and state governments would need to be significantly improved and expanded. Joint communication messages could be established and strategically played out in the target markets important for Germany.

Bibliography

Anholt-Ipsos Nation Brands Index (NBI). (2019) *Germany Retains Top "Nation Brand" Ranking, France and Canada Emerge to Round Out the Top Three.* IPSOS.

Bennett, W. L. (1998) The Uncivic Culture: Communication, Identity, and the Rise of Lifestyle Politics. *PS: Political Science and Politics,* 31, 741–761.

Bergler, R. (2008) Identität und Image. In Günter Bentele, Romy Fröhlich, and Peter Szyszka (Hg.), *Handbuch der Public Relations* (pp. 321–334). Wissenschaftliche Grundlagen und berufliches Handeln, Wiesbaden.

Christensen, C. (1997) *The Innovator's Dilemma: When New Technologies Cause Great Firms to Fail.* Harvard Business Review Press, Cambridge, MA.

German Association for International Cooperation (GIZ). (2018) *Germany in the Eyes of the World.* Retrieved from https://www.giz.de/en/worldwide/63709.html

IPSOS. (2020, October 27). *Germany Retains Top "Nation Brand" Ranking, US and China Experience Significant Decline* [Press release]. Retrieved from https://www.ipsos.com/en-us/news-polls/Germany-Retains-Top-Nation-Brand-Ranking-the-United-Kingdom-emerges-ahead-of-Canada-to-Round-Out-the-Top-Three-US-and-China-Experience-Significant-Decline

Nye Jr, J. S. (2005) *Soft Power: The Means to Success in World Politics* (New ed.). Public Affairs, New York.

Schwan, A. (2011) *Werbung statt Waffen.* VS Verlag für Sozialwissenschaften. Springer.

World Economic Forum. (2018) *The Global Competitiveness Report.*

Zimmermann, O., and Geißler, T. (Eds.). (2018) *Die dritte Säule: Auswärtige Kultur-und Bildungspolitik* (Vol. 16). Deutscher Kulturrat eV, Berlin.

3 France

Christophe Alaux[1]

Branding France or branding France(s): from nation branding to local branding

Nation branding applies branding and marketing communications techniques to promote a nation's image (Fan, 2006). Despite its reputation and its image, France is behind neighbouring countries with regard to current place marketing targets such as the number of investors and talent attraction. Beyond its strengths, much work has to be done to manage such a national brand with so many cities and regions which already manage their brands on their own (18 regions, 101 counties and 34,970 municipalities). Indeed, city and regional marketing is highly developed in France with significant place branding at the local level.

For an analysis of the French case, we use a classic methodology developed by place marketing practitioners (Chamard and Alaux, 2018) as follows:

- Diagnostic of the place and the brand
- Vision and governance of place attractiveness
- Strategic and operational place marketing
- Evaluation and recommendations.

Diagnostic: a strong brand in need of reinvention

France is a brand with strong results, but deeper analysis also shows some weaknesses, especially when compared with top international brands.

As the world's top tourism destination with its 89.3 million foreign visitors in 2018, France is a very attractive destination for neighbouring European countries, which represent 70 million of its foreign visitors in 2018. However, it is worth noting that between 15 million and 20 million tourists only visit France because they are on their way towards other destinations;

DOI: 10.4324/9781003084051-3

this may explain a duration significantly shorter than the average stay in neighbouring countries with an average length of stay of 6.7 nights in 2018.[2] France is also a strong place for foreign direct investors with 1,323 investment decisions and 30,302 jobs created or maintained in 2018.[3]

Despite its strong results, France has encountered some difficulties in competing with top countries. The analysis of France's brand image in international surveys and rankings confirms this diagnostic. For instance, France is seen as a powerful brand. Indeed, it is ranked in second position, after Germany, in the Nation Brand Index for 2019.[4] Over the last decade, France has consistently placed in the top 5 of this ranking. According to the Kantar Public/Business France survey, France ranks as the second-best European country for investors, second only to Germany.[5]

However, other rankings are not as positive. The FutureBrand 2011–2012 study ranked France 17th out of 113 countries for its value system, 18th for its quality of life and 16th for its business opportunities. In 2020, FutureBrand ranked France 14th out of 75 countries. The 2014/2015 Country Brand Index study ranked France in a median position both for positive experiences (tourism, history and culture, strength of 'made in') and for mental representations (value system, quality of life, business attractiveness). Contrary to countries such as Japan, Germany or Switzerland, according to the Country Brand Index, France lacks a strong country brand, particularly due to its low average score on the dimension of purpose (quality of life, business potential, value system). More worrying still is France's absence from the top ten places for all elements related to the mental representations it inspires. As a result, these rankings emphasize the need for France to reinvent its brand image in order to compete with other strong country brands.

But why should the world's leading nation brand (for tourism) reinvent itself? Of course, France has strong assets that are widely known: the richness and diversity of its landscapes, its history and culture, as well as its exceptional geographical location. But, the absence of a founding myth around the French economy puts the country at a disadvantage. Indeed, France does not have a well-recognized and shared historical economic narrative. Its founding myths are mainly political, social and cultural.[6] Moreover, studies show that technology and innovation will increasingly define country brands; this represents a change in the perception of country brands that were previously defined by political, economic and cultural factors. Today's image of France does not match with these technological and innovative dimensions. Its brand equity does not seem to be adapted to the expectations of the future. The only two French companies ranked among the world's top 50 brands show little added value in terms of technology: L'Oréal and LVMH. Unsurprisingly, this result is in line with the close association between country brands and the perception of their areas of expertise. France is mostly associated with fashion for 65% of respondents, while Japan is associated with technology for 78%.[7] Ultimately, France needs to acknowledge that its image and the quality of its brand are not the only reasons for its status as the world's leading tourist destination. In marketing, a powerful brand is a strong determinant of performance because it brings together a set of affective, emotional and symbolic elements which create value for the consumer, beyond the product itself. But the branding of nations and places is not a copy of corporate branding (Kavaratzis, 2009). If we follow Fan, a main difference lies in the benefits that a nation brand can create for its audience: they are emotional rather than functional (Fan, 2006).

Governance and vision

In 2013, the France brand was evaluated by a board of experts directed by Philippe Lentschener. A report and a charter of the France brand were elaborated with 20 recommendations to improve the competitiveness of the France brand (Gardel, 2013). One recommendation was the merger of all attractiveness agencies (FDI, Tourism, Talent Attraction Agency) in a single E.I.G.[8] Despite this recommendation and the best intentions to manage France as a global brand with a single governance structure, 7 years later, the current governance is still comprised of a network of many sectorial actors at the national level. Acting closely with the Ministry of Foreign Affairs and the Secretary of Tourism, Atout France is the national E.I.G.[9] in charge of France as a destination. It manages the website www.france. fr and a new destination brand 'Explore France' that was launched in 2019. In 2013, destination contracts were implemented to label destinations at the local level and to promote them internationally. Working jointly with the Ministry of the Economy and Finance, Business France is the national E.I.G.[10] that promotes France as a location for investors and as an exporter. It manages the brand 'Choose France' and the website: www.welcometofrance.fr. Different branding and network organizations function under the brand umbrella 'Choose France,' such as French Tech, a highly active network to promote French startups abroad.[11]

Marketing strategy/positioning

The brand France is aimed at multiple targets: tourists, investors, talent, students and so on. Instead of one clear positioning, the brand has focused on different positioning in the economic and touristic sectors. France has been branded in isolation as a destination and as an economic brand, but it should be managed as a global brand instead of advancing these two dimensions in isolation. In fact, just as international cities compete with each other in terms of global attractiveness (companies, mega-events, investors, talents, tourists, students, etc.), country brands are also transitioning towards a more global mentality, leaving behind their former function as sectorial brands. Recent literature highlights the need to develop research into the relationship between nation branding and foreign direct investment (FDI) in order to evaluate the effectiveness of global nation brands (Hao et al., 2019). Having a strong global nation brand may give a competitive advantage in terms of tourism, investment and consumer preferences for the country's products and services. However, it is hard to communicate the same positioning for different international targets, whether tourists or investors in industries as diverse as the automotive sector, aeronautics, fashion or healthcare. Choosing a similar positioning for all audiences or different positioning for different audiences can lead to meaningless perceptions for targets (Fan, 2006). Moreover, this positioning should also be meaningful for internal targets: a country's citizens (Che-Ha et al., 2016).

In the last 10 years, targeting strategies for France have been increasingly differentiated, with separate initiatives in tourism and FDI to promote the brand France:

- 2013: Destination contracts: The Ministry of Foreign Affairs launched a bid for regional and local French destinations to be identified and communicated at the international level with Atout France. Around 20 French destinations are certificated with a 3-year contract between all destination stakeholders.
- 2014: French Tech[12]: this new economic branding aimed at promoting the technological and digital French ecosystem abroad. Different regional and metropolitan French tech areas were certificated 'French Tech' to communicate abroad with a single voice on those topics.
- 2017: Welcome to France: this platform was launched by Business France to attract international talent.
- 2019: Bienvenue en France: Foreign students were targeted with a specific national programme that is delivered in several universities which were certified according to relevant criteria. This benchmark for quality is managed by the Ministry of Higher Education, Research and Innovation.

The future of nation branding for France

For many authors, the France brand should capitalize on its reputation for elegance, its gastronomy, its landscapes and its historical and cultural prestige. As Magnusson et al. (2019, p. 16) showed in their empirical study of product country of origin, 'brand managers can use COO personality stereotypes to their advantage'. Indeed, for external consumers, a brand positioning which is coherent with COO stereotypes would lead to more favourable evaluations for the product. By extension to the French case, it could mean strengthening the relationship between the France brand and the characteristics of the Paris brand. The proximity of image for France and Paris is obvious 'given the weight and characteristics of the image of Paris and its international rankings' (Margot-Duclot, 2011, p. 68). Jean-Noël Kapferer also suggests focusing on these stereotypes 'and then put it at the service of a brand mission: quality growth for all' (Kapferer, 2011, p. 139).

Others argue that the brand should position itself as a balanced combination of French creativity and technology. A 2013 report[13] on the France brand suggests that 'creativity and imagination are the primary agents of a competitive economy'. In this way, the French brand would be dissociated from its stereotypical, external image. In light of the evolution of the perceptions of country brands that are anchored on the dimensions of technology and innovation, this positioning seems more a response to a global expectation than a real positioning based on a proven territorial identity. However, place identity must remain the foundation of the place brand. To reconcile identity and image, we could therefore focus on positioning French innovation and technology to enrich identity stereotypes related to gastronomy, lifestyle, luxury, fashion and so on. This would make it possible to avoid too strong a dissociation between the external image, the identity of the territory and the positioning of the brand.

Regarding the way to establish a new France brand policy, Kapferer considers that it can only exist through 'the visibility and impact of its products insofar as they are consistent with the brand platform and values' (Kapferer, 2011, pp. 151–152). However, at a national level, territorial brand policies cannot adopt the franchising logic of commercial brands. Territories are 'too complex to be treated as products' (Kavaratzis and Ashworth, 2005, p. 510) or trademarks (Alaux et al., 2016; Kavaratzis, 2004). The transposition of marketing in the public sector has been the subject of much debate among both those who argue that marketing is not scalable and those who argue that the public sector is not very responsive (Alaux, 2018). The concept of place branding and reputation has, however, been adapted to the national level (Kotler et al., 2002; Alaux et al., 2020). A growing body of scientific literature over the last 20 years has also made it possible to draw up a state of the art for branding cities (Lucarelli and Berg, 2011; Vuignier, 2018). In light of these contributions, France has a dilemma for its national brand, with so many strong international brands at the local level and the difficulty of giving meaning to this diversity under a single brand umbrella.

On the basis of this triple observation, we put forward three recommendations:

- The France brand should not attempt to change the stereotypical perception, which would deprive it of the status of a strong country brand;
- The France brand must exploit its assets linked to technology and innovation which correspond to its real identity;
- The France brand cannot impose a uniform brand policy on its different territories.

If the objective is indeed to make France a strong brand that will ensure its overall attractiveness, it must be noted that some of its territories embody these dimensions better than France itself. By associating their territorial brands with the France brand, it could therefore help to change the perception of France. According to Michel Saint-Pé,[14] Director of the Moselle Place Marketing Agency (Moselle is on the border of France and Germany),

> territories can in particular associate profitable cross-border images. Moselle thus plays on this "dual culture" by highlighting the positive aspects of the German economy: product quality, mastery of cutting-edge technologies, a training system "sticking" to the needs of businesses, a culture of social dialogue, commercial dynamism, which often enables us to mitigate some of the negative points of the French image.

Consequently, the France brand must be based on the identity and image of its attractive territories around a hybrid positioning based on very enduring national stereotypes and innovative dimensions at the local level. The Provence destination contract combines this hybrid dimension through a heritage ('art de vivre and heritage, art de vivre and heritage of taste') and a contemporary ('art de vivre and culture of the living') identity.

Relying on this does not mean using it as a tool. The objective would be to share the France brand, by involving and networking these attractive territories so that they carry the France brand and enrich it with dimensions that it is not able to promote on its own.

It is therefore necessary to reinvent the France brand: to make it a hybrid, shared destination brand based on its relevant and attractive territories, in the sense of place marketing.

The common point of these territories is their notoriety and the strong richness of positive representations they inspire, especially on the technological/innovation dimensions. It should be remembered, for example, that

Paris, Lyon, Marseille, Bordeaux and Nice are cities regularly recognized for their innovative character.

The France brand could thus be used as 'an inspirational catalyst who aims to coordinate actions under its umbrella' (Kapferer, 2011, p. 151). France as a whole would be the central inspirational nucleus of a France brand (Michel, 1999), enriched by peripheral nuclei carrying innovative and technological dimensions that are expected by some target audiences (Chamard et al., 2013). Michel Saint-Pé[15] puts forward the idea that territories play this role: 'by presenting our key strengths (industrial and tertiary sector flagships, competitiveness clusters, grandes écoles, major tourist and cultural sites, etc.), we actively participate in the influence and attractiveness of the French product'. According to Isabelle Brémond, 'Under the banner of France, the Provence brand aims to develop the attractiveness of the region and to promote the destination'.[16] The relationship between the central brand and the peripheral brands must be carefully analysed in all these multilateral relationships.

Moreover, city and regional marketing are much utilized by French local authorities. Large-sized cities have a strong image and develop strategies for global markets (Benko, 1999; Zenker and Beckmann, 2013). But place marketing is also used by small-sized cities (SSC) which often suffer from a poor image and have the greatest difficulty in attracting and retaining residents or investors. For the specific case of France, collaboration between all local (SSC, metropolitan areas, counties, regions) and national organizations is crucial to improve the management of the nation brand image (Fan, 2010). As such, this focus on collaboration would follow the marketing discipline evolution with its shift from value distribution to value creation and from a focus on outcome to a focus on process (Sheth and Parvatiyar, 1995).

The question of nation branding for France raises both political and managerial interrogations:

- A political issue for the governance of the brand at the national level: how can the governance of the France brand be streamlined and simplified in the future? Many Ministries (and State Secretaries) and Agencies are involved in managing the brand with a clear separation between two sectors of activities: economic investment/talent attraction targets and tourism targets. In 2013, the recommendation to merge agencies to manage the brand into a single entity was not implemented. The leadership of two major Ministries (Foreign Affairs and Economy) may explain the difficulty in merging these agencies and developing a more understandable governance for the brand.
- A managerial issue: Should France be a very visible shared global brand utilized by all famous local brands? Or should it be limited

to a more managerial role of coordination between all famous local brands? Before answering this issue, two strategic questions must be answered:

- Does France need to be promoted as a global brand in a logic of cross-sectorial attractiveness (trade, tourism, events, talent attraction, higher education, diplomacy) that corresponds to the approaches implemented today by the most attractive metropolitan areas?
- Does France need to benefit from the attractiveness of its best performing places (cities and regions), in particular in terms of technology and innovation?

Answering simultaneously all these questions is not an easy task. Finding strategic answers will require a clearer definition of the nation brand that France will seek to embody in the years to come.

Notes

1 The author strongly thanks Flora Macivor, Professeur Agrégé at IMPGT (Aix Marseille University), for her precious help in improving the writing of this chapter.
2 Insee, 2019 : www.entreprises.gouv.fr/files/files/directions_services/etudes-et-statistiques/4p-DGE/2019-07-4Pn88-EVE.pdf
3 Business France Report (2018): https://world.businessfrance.fr/nordic/wp-content/uploads/sites/903/2016/04/BFP-2019-Annual-report-Foreign-investment-in-France.pdf
4 Source: www.ipsos.com/sites/default/files/chart-anholt.png
5 Source: Business France (www.businessfrance.fr/discover-france-news-france-attractiveness-survey-2019): 'France remains Europe's second most attractive country after Germany but ahead of the United Kingdom: it is cited by 38% of the executives surveyed, compared with 44% in favor of Germany and 30% in favor of the United Kingdom.'
6 France Brand Report (2013): www.entreprises.gouv.fr/files/files/directions_services/politique-et-enjeux/competitivite/marque-france/rapport-marque-france-2013-06-28.pdf
7 The Future Brand Index, Future Brand, 2014.
8 Economic Interest Grouping (EIG) : Agency with public/private partnership.
9 Ibid.
10 Ibid.
11 https://lafrenchtech.com/fr/
12 https://lafrenchtech.com/en/
13 France Brand Report (2013): www.entreprises.gouv.fr/files/files/directions_services/politique-et-enjeux/competitivite/marque-france/rapport-marque-france-2013-06-28.pdf
14 Interview for French Chair 'New Place Marketing and Attractiveness", 2017

15 Director of Moselle Place marketing Agency (Moselle Attractivité), Interview for French Chair 'New Place Marketing and Attractiveness", 2017.

16 Director of Provence Destination Management Organization (Provence Tourisme), Interview for French Chair 'New Place Marketing and Attractiveness", 2017.

References

Alaux, C. (2018) *Vers un management public créateur de valeur : les nouveaux apports du marketing public à l'attractivité des territoires*. Habilitation à diriger les recherches. Institut de Management Public et Gouvernance Territoriale, Aix-Marseille-Université.

Alaux, C., Carmouze, L., and Serval, S. (2020) What's in a Place Name: Reputation Components and Drivers. A Comparison of Five European Metropolises' Perceptions. *Management international-Mi*, 24(spécial), 139–149.

Alaux, C., Serval, S., and Zeller, C. (2016) Le marketing territorial des Petits et Moyens Territoires : identité, image et relations. *Gestion et Management Public*, 4(2), 61–78.

Benko, G. (1999) Marketing et territoire. In Fontan, J. M., Klein, J. L. and Tremblay, D. G. (Eds.), *Entre la métropolisation et le village globale* (pp. 79–122). Presses de l'Université du Québec, Québec.

Chamard, C., and Alaux, C. (2018) Place Hospitality: A Way to Understand and Improve Place Marketing Approaches. *International Journal of Management Science and Business Administration*, 4(2), 7–16.

Chamard, C., Liquet, J. C., and Mengi, M. (2013) L'image de marque des régions françaises : évaluation du " capital territoire " par le grand public. *Revue Française Du Marketing*, 244/245(4/5–5), 27–43.

Che-Ha, N., Nguyen, B., Yahya, W. K., Melewar, T. C., and Chen, Y. P. (2016) Country Branding Emerging from Citizens' Emotions and the Perceptions of Competitive Advantage: The Case of Malaysia. *Journal of Vacation Marketing*, 22(1).

Fan, Y. (2006) Branding the Nation: What Is Being Branded? *Journal of Vacation Marketing*, 12(1), 5–14.

Fan, Y. (2010) Branding the Nation: Towards a Better Understanding. *Place Branding and Public Diplomacy*, 6(2), 97–103.

Gardel, M. (2013) La Marque France. *Géoéconomie*, 4(67), 45–56.

Hao, A. W., Paul, J., Trott, S., Guo, C., and Wu, H. H. (2019) Two Decades of Research on Nation Branding: A Review and Future Research Agenda. *International Marketing Review*, 38(1), 46–69.

Kapferer. (2011) Quelle stratégie pour la marque France, demain? https://doi.org/10.3166/RFG.218-219.139-153.

Kavaratzis, M. (2004) From City Marketing to City Branding: Towards a Theoretical Framework for Developing City Brands. *Place Branding*, 1(1), 58–73.

Kavaratzis, M. (2009) Cities and Their Brands: Lessons from Corporate Branding. *Place Branding and Public Diplomacy*, 5(1), 26–37.

Kavaratzis, M., and Ashworth, G. J. (2005) City Branding: An Effective Assertion of Identity or a Transitory Marketing Trick? *Tijdschrift Voor Economische En Sociale Geografie*, 96(5), 506–514.

Kotler, P., Haider, D., and Rein, I. (2002) *Marketing Places: Attracting Investment, Industry And Tourism To Cities, States and Nations.* The Free Press.

Lucarelli, A., and Berg, P. O. (2011) City Branding: A State-of-the-Art Review of the Research Domain. *Journal of Place Management and Development*, 4(1), 9–27.

Magnusson, P., Westjohn, S. A., and Sirianni, N. J. (2019) Beyond Country Image Favorability: How Brand Positioning via Country Personality Stereotypes Enhances Brand Evaluations. *Journal of International Business Studies*, 50(3), 318–338.

Michel, G. (1999) L'évolution des marques: approche par la théorie du noyau central. *Recherche et Applications En Marketing*, 14(4), 33–53.

Sheth, J. N., and Parvatiyar, A. (1995) The Evolution of Relationship Marketing. *International Business Review*, 4(4), 397–418.

Vuignier, R. (2018) *Attractivité des territoires et place branding : étude exploratoire de la sensibilité des décideurs d'entreprise à la marque territoriale*, 277. https://serval.unil.ch/resource/serval:BIB_7B2F6FF7B3E0.P001/REF.

Zenker, S., and Beckmann, S. C. (2013) My Place Is Not Your Place – Different Place Brand Knowledge by Different Target Groups. *Journal of Place Management and Development*, 6(1), 6–17.

4 United Kingdom

Malcolm Allan

Introduction

The focus of this chapter is on the United Kingdom. More specifically, it is an exploration of why the country does not currently have a nation brand strategy, the challenges it will face if it decides to create one and the prospects of it deciding to do so.

For the purposes of this exploration I define nation brand strategy as a process for describing the present offer of a country for its citizens, what it offers to the rest of the world and, most importantly, its vision for its future development of those offers and the experience of living in the country, visiting the country and dealing with the country; in short how the country is seen and wants to be seen by its citizens and by people in the rest of the world and how this aspiration is defined, the big idea that defines the future of the country and how it will be achieved.

Does the UK have a nation brand strategy?

The short answer is no.

However, the United Kingdom does have a brand by which I mean that it has an identity as a country that is recognized to a greater or lesser extent around the world depending on people's knowledge and understanding of the country, what it offers them and their experience of being there or dealing with it. This identity, formed by people's perceptions of the country has, over the last 10 years, been highly rated by a number of brand rating and valuation indexes.[1] However, rankings such as these have been questioned[2] as only offering a snapshot picture of a country at one point in time, whereas the reputation of a country or nation is built over time and influenced by a myriad of factors. The ranking tools I am most familiar with, those of Bloom Consulting, have as their primary objective the measurement the impact international perceptions and reputations may have *over time* on each country brand.

DOI: 10.4324/9781003084051-4

The 2019 Bloom Index for International Trade[3] ranked the United Kingdom as second globally after the United States and the absolute leader in Europe. The United Kingdom established this solid position due to a higher Average Net FDI inflow and a robust indicator of Digital Demand – D2© (second in Europe, sixth in the world) with a strong online presence indicating that the 2016 Brexit referendum seems to have not yet affected the reputation of the United Kingdom, although its effects will be truly seen in future rankings for 2020–2023 after the country has exited the European Union and what kind of exit it had.

So, even although the United Kingdom has never had a nation brand development strategy, it has a strongly ranked brand offer for trade and a similarly strong offer for its current tourism offer. Why is this the case? In large part it may be due to the success of what is known as the 'Great Campaign'. This is a country marketing campaign whose graphic identity is a logo based on the words 'Great' and 'Britain' whose purpose is to promote the many and varied things that Britain is good or great at, its offers of value to its citizens and the wider world.

The 'Great Britain' campaign

Established in 2012 the overall vision for the Great Campaign was to inspire the world to think and feel differently about the United Kingdom now and in the future, demonstrating that it is the best nation 'to visit, to invest in, trade with and study in'.[4] The Great Britain Campaign is the UK government's major initiative to promote the country as a destination for tourists, trade and investment and students in order to secure economic growth. As such, the campaign seeks to promote the United Kingdom's unique selling points including innovation, creativity, technology, entrepreneurs, heritage, culture, countryside, shopping, luxury, food, music and knowledge.

Before the campaign began in 2012 there was no consistent approach to the promotion of the United Kingdom overseas. Instead, UK government departments promoted the United Kingdom using their own brands, logos and names. And, regional bodies in England promoted their regions using different brands, effectively competing with each other in the same foreign markets.

In consequence, there was little coordination between tourism, trade and investment and education institutions when promoting the United Kingdom overseas.

Responsibility for the campaign sits with the Cabinet Office in No. 10 Downing Street in London governed under a Great Campaign Board with staffing from the Cabinet office, making use of the 'convening power' and influence of the Prime Minister.

The establishment of the campaign involved creating the logo, design, guidelines and images, developing a strategy and allocating funding. Great delivery partners use the materials developed as the basis for overseas marketing campaigns and online to reach target audiences to try to change their perceptions of the country. Thus, it provides an integrated and consistent marketing platform for international promotion efforts of key central government departments, for example the Department for International Trade, The Foreign and Commonwealth Office, VisitBritain and the British Council. It was the first time that the UK government had attempted to unify its efforts to promote the country in a coordinated way.[5] In more detail this involved:

- Coordination of 21 government departments and arms-length bodies
- Activity in 144 countries and 252 diplomatic posts, particularly in the key markets of Brazil, China, India and the United States
- Delivery of 80–100 economic activities and programmes each month
- Recruitment of 200-plus private sector partners and 164 high profile individuals and £68 million in sponsorship, enabling partners to do more in their target markets
- Provision to partners of strong and effective marketing tools
- Evaluation by outcomes of activity and tangible investments rather than volume of activity or intention to invest.

A review of the campaign published in 2015[6] estimated that it had achieved a return of £1.2 billion on an investment of £113.5 million. By 2017 the return on the investment was estimated at £1.77 billion and within this figure the return for trade was investment of £720 million.

As successful as the Great Campaign has been it is not a UK nation brand strategy. For example, it does not convey to the citizens of the United Kingdom and the rest of the world what kind of country its governments want the United Kingdom to become, in particular post-Brexit (fully leaving the EU) beyond 2021, and an agreed shared vision for the future development of the country.

Almost all of the nation brand development strategies that I have worked on since 2002 have been focused on an agreed shared vision within the country among the populace on the kind of place it wants to be by a future date, being implemented through a detailed strategy and action plan to move from their current reality to their desired future state. No such conversation has taken place within the United Kingdom and a unified vision for the United Kingdom has yet to emerge.

The prospects for a 'Global Britain'

However, there has been much discussion of the idea of a 'Global Britain' emerging after Brexit is completed but no agreement on what this might mean between the Parliament in Westminster and the devolved administrations in Northern Ireland, Scotland and Wales; in fact, there are a variety of viewpoints on what this term might mean.

In 2020, the UK Prime Minister, Boris Johnson, and his ministers talked about 'Global Britain' without really defining precisely what they mean by those two words.

The reaction to Global Britain when the phrase was first coined was hostile.[7] The UK Parliament's Foreign Affairs Committee[8] judged that Global Britain risked being a mere 'slogan' devoid of substance. And Peter Ricketts, a former FCO Permanent Under-Secretary, in Prospect[9] asserted that Global Britain 'would do little to solve the question of Britain's world role'. A report into the take-up of Global Britain at the United Nations[10] surmised that 'there is still no clarity on what Global Britain might mean even from a UK perspective'.

More precisely and comprehensively 'Making Global Britain Work' published in 2019 by the Policy Exchange[11] set out eight ideas for revitalising UK foreign policy for the post-Brexit age, developed by the 'Britain in the World Initiative' to revitalise the British foreign policy debate in the United Kingdom, to challenge the narrative of decline, encourage the creation of a new generation of foreign policy leaders and to ask hard questions about Britain's place in the world, its hard and soft power assets and future grand strategy.

In summary, the eight ideas concern the way the United Kingdom thinks about and conducts its foreign policy, what the Policy Exchange terms as 'creative conservative internationalism,' ideas to change the way we think about national security, prepare ourselves better for the new age of competition, stay ahead as the most important player in European defence, develop a prudent strategy for an active role in the Indo-Pacific region, retain humanitarian goals as an irreducible component of UK foreign policy, and create a dedicated 'British Future Unit' in No 10 alongside a new Cabinet sub-committee chaired by the Prime Minister. However, important as these ideas are, this is not is a comprehensive characterization of a Global Britain, a future Britain other than in foreign policy terms, though the idea for a British Future Unit is worth considering as a place to develop a wider definition of a future United Kingdom.

More recently, perhaps in an attempt to provide clarity on the meaning of 'Global Britain,' published on 23 September 2019 on the UK Government website (www.gov.uk), is a page that states that its purpose is to bring together materials that set out the UK government's vision for Global Britain. This list contains the Prime Minister's speeches, the Foreign Secretary's announcements and The National Security Capability Review. So, it is a set of ideas and pronouncements by key cabinet ministers based on existing or proposed government policy statements and it is party political.

A key statement on the web page recognizes that the pace of change in the world, shifts in the global context (undefined), and a new relationship with Europe, will all have an impact on how the UK government projects influence and protects its national interests. It goes on to state that Global Britain is about investing in our relationships, championing the rules-based international order and demonstrating that the United Kingdom is open, outward-looking and confident on the world stage.

What the statement does not do is to spell out the kind of place the country wants to become in the future and how it is going to get there. It is not based on a national conversation or a national consensus. It does not present a comprehensive view of the United Kingdom's future role in the world. It is a partial view of our future – a view of our ability to trade successfully with the rest of the world. It is not a comprehensive nation brand development strategy.

However, I believe that 2020/21, as we leave the EU, presents the constituent countries of the United Kingdom with an opportunity to develop collective thinking on what they want a future United Kingdom to be like, what it would be good at, what it would offer its people, what they would like to be known for and liked for. Beyond the vacuous and limited explanations for Global Britain, one scenario that has been mooted is that the country should invest in the development of a more resilient, sustainable and greener economy as the basis for its recovery from the Coronavirus pandemic. But will the devolved administrations of the United Kingdom in Northern Ireland, Scotland and Wales want to work with the Westminster Parliament and the current government of the United Kingdom to develop a unified nation brand strategy for the country on this basis? Will the current government wish to do so?

The prospects for the development of a UK nation brand strategy?

Despite the 'Great Campaign,' at present in the United Kingdom there are many brand-based or branded strategies for marketing and promoting the offers of the United Kingdom as a whole and of its constituent nations; a smorgasbord of branded strategies, marketing and promotion plans and campaigns that, to an outsider, is likely to be confusing.

In addition to the 'Great' campaign there is the VisitBritain tourism development strategy, the VisitEngland tourism development strategy and associated marketing, the Visit Wales tourism development strategy and the associated Wales Brand destination marketing strategy, the National Economic Development Strategy of the Welsh Assembly Government, the strategy of Trade and Invest Wales, the VisitScotland tourism development strategy and the 'Scotland Is Now' campaign, the Northern Ireland Tourism Development Strategy, the Tourism Ireland Marketing campaign jointly run with The Republic of Ireland and the Invest Northern Ireland Business Strategy and associated marketing.

Of all of these initiatives the 'Scotland Is Now'[12] campaign is the one that most closely resembles the focus, integration and coordination of the Great campaign and the one that has the most potential to become a proper nation brand strategy.

In a number of ways, the progress made on devolution of government within the United Kingdom to its constituent nations, bar England, which remains firmly under the governance of the Westminster Parliament, has created major challenges for the prospects of there being a nation brand strategy for the United Kingdom. These challenges include:

(1) The progress that the devolved administrations have made on developing policies and strategies for their implementation within their countries;
(2) The establishment of recognized brands (strategies and logos) for the development of their tourism, investment and economic development activities and offers;
(3) The growing sense of individual country identities that this activity has created internationally which has served to re-emphasize their individual country heritage and cultures;
(4) The unease created by the differences in policies related to the handling of the COVID-19 pandemic between the devolved nations and those of the UK government at Westminster.
(5) The combative nature of UK politics where party manifestos prioritize partial and disparate visions of the UK for a parliamentary 5-year period, a process that effectively currently prohibits any prospect of there being a consensus on what kind of country the people of the UK nations want it to be.

In consequence, the prospects for there being a national conversation about what kind of country its people want it to be, to be known for and their vision for life here in the future are slim, not least because there are appearing distinctly different visions among the administrations about what should be to focus of the economic recovery from the pandemic.

Is there any prospect that we can move on from party political manifesto visions of the next 5 years to a genuine cross-party, fully involving (of people) conversation on a medium-term (10 years?) vision for the development of the country and nation post-Brexit and post-pandemic?

Possibly not as an opportunity to have a national conversation about this has effectively been squandered by the government at Westminster publishing its post-pandemic economic recovery 'Build, Build, Build' strategy without any meaningful, realistic and relevant conversation with the devolved administrations.

This could have been an opportunity to move on from the divisions of Brexit and frame a new vision for the country based on how we rebuild our economy in a sustainable, green way, as a meaningful response to the climate emergency, as a number of commentators have been advocating.[13]

A recent post on the Carbon Brief website[14] presented new research,[15] based on surveys of more than 200 of the world's most senior economists and economic officials, identified five stand-out policy measures for a green recovery: clean physical infrastructure investment; building-efficiency spending; investment in education and training; natural capital investment for ecosystem resilience and clean R&D spending.

These are measures that do not figure sufficiently or prominently in the UK government's policy for recovery but which may do so in the responses of the devolved administrations and which may presage the emergence of comprehensive nation-branding strategies for their countries which, if developed, may leave England without one.

So, in conclusion, to coin an analogy, if the United Kingdom were a large multi-department retail store house, like Harrods or Selfridges in London it has the options of drawing the departments together into one brand strategy and offer (unlikely) or remaining a 'House of Brands,' possibly complementary, but don't bank on it.

If there was a willingness among the devolved administrations and the Westminster parliament to work together on the creation of a UK country brand development strategy, from our experience of advising governments elsewhere on doing so, a number of requirements need to be met if such work is to be taken seriously and result in an agreed approach. These include:

• Establishing widespread trust among the population that the governments know what they are doing
• Establishing a truly national conversation on the kind of country we aspire to be and how to realize that vision, a conversation not governed

by or hidebound by party political manifestos or by the dominance of the Westminster Parliament

- Identifying a 'Central Idea' on what will define the United Kingdom of the future, one that will help drive and guide its longer-term recovery from the pandemic
- Perhaps by establishing a 'Green, Sustainable and Resilient Nations Alliance' to take forward this work.

Notes

1 For example, the annual Brand Indexes of Anholt-GfK Roper, Bloom Consulting and FutureBrand.
2 https://placebrandobserver.com/country-brand-rankings/
3 www.bloom-consulting.com/en/pdf/rankings/Bloom_Consulting_Country_Brand_Ranking_Trade.pdf
4 www.greatbritaincampaign.com/
5 Conrad Bird, former Director of the Great Campaign, Civil Service Quarterly, August 2017.
6 'Exploiting the UK Brand Overseas', National Audit office, June 2015.
7 Oliver Daddow, Assistant Professor of Politics, University of Nottingham, LSE Blog (blogs.lse.ac.uk), April 2019.
8 Global Britain, House of Commons Foreign Affairs Committee, Sixth Report of Session 2017–2019.
9 'Why Brexit means diminished British weight in the world', 6 May 2018.
10 'Global Britain in The United Nations', Jess Gifkins, Samual Jarvie and Jason Ralph, February 2019.
11 'Making Global Britain Work – 8 ideas for revitalising UK foreign policy for the post-Brexit age', The Britain in the World Project at Policy Exchange, 2019.
12 www.scotlandisnow.com
13 www.carbonbrief.org/leading-economists-green-coronavirus-recovery-also-better-for-economy 05.05.2020.
14 Brian O'Callaghan and Prof Cameron Hepburn on 05.05,2020.
15 'Will Covid-19 fiscal recovery accelerate or retard progress on climate change?' – Cameron Hepburn et al, Working Paper No 20–02 Oxford Smith School of Enterprise and the Environment, 04.05.2020.

5 Italy

Cecilia Pasquinelli

1. Insights into Italy's brand reputation

Italy's brand reputation is deeply rooted in heritage, culture and 'Made in' products, particularly luxury fashion products (FutureBrand Country Index, 2019). Creative goods export has been confirmed as a salient component of the country's national projection into the global scene (Good Country Index, 2019). Data has confirmed strong brand awareness and positive response to the brand, while internally a negative sentiment about the country and what it can offer through critical economic phases seems to prevail amongst Italians, although significant differences emerge across the peninsula (Symbola, 2017).

There is room to speak of brand equity since not only is the brand easily recognized but positive judgements and feelings have emerged in a recent survey, with significant propensity to make repeat visits to the country amongst those that already visited, revealing a long-term relationship with the brand (Symbola, 2017). Quality of life connected with places, food, creativity and culture are confirmed core brand associations. Tourism is an important dimension of Italy's country brand, with attractions and food playing a crucial role (1st global position in the FutureBrand Country Index, 2012).

While science and technology dimensions tend not to be in sharp focus in respondents' perceptions of Italy, innovation and cutting-edge results are perceived in relation to the food and wine offering, which is associated with excellence in sustainability, empowerment of local communities, well-being and authenticity (Symbola, 2017).

2. Nation brand 'structure': FDI promotion, made in Italy and the destination brand

Italy's brand 'structure' is composed of different sub-brands pertaining to different fields in which the national image exerts its power. However, there

DOI: 10.4324/9781003084051-5

is no brand architecture that strategically defines the different brand roles and relationships (Aaker and Joachimsthaler, 2000). As much branding literature suggests, brand architecture is fundamental to provide synergy and leverage and to avoid brand potential remaining untapped and value creation opportunities being missed. The lack of a branding strategy is evident in the Italian case: the inherited brand equity – nurtured over time through the contributions of several protagonists of the arts, culture and business in national history – is exploited, but limited strategic effort has been made to maintain and enhance the nation brand.

Nevertheless, it is true that various communication and promotional campaigns have been developed over time, attempting to promote Italy in the FDI market, in the tourism market and in international consumer markets in which national manufacturing industries built their reputation. The strong and positive perception of national cultural heritage plays a role in constructing the competitive advantage of culture-related products and services (Napolitano and De Nisco, 2017).

Despite the absence of an integrated nation branding strategy, an underlying brand value proposition consistently emerged, which refers to beauty (*Bel Paese*), know-how and creativity (*bello e ben fatto*) rooted in the Italian cultural heritage (often the Renaissance heritage is used as a repository of values and imagery). This convergence derives from a consolidated practice of communicating the nation that levers fairly stereotypical brand associations. Although credible, familiar and meaningful to global audiences and, accordingly, representing important brand knowledge, these associations have often failed to convey innovative attributes and values and have missed the opportunity to explain meaningful links between the past and country heritage, and contemporary Italian culture, society and economy.

The fact that the Italy brand has a strong potential and a reputation that has remained largely unmanaged is not a novelty. Rather, this is fairly consolidated knowledge following several analyses, studies and long-standing debate involving entrepreneurs, politicians and academics. Consequently, it is important to reflect on the reasons that have kept the nation brand in an immaturity stage. One possible reason resides in the brand governance which has remained highly fragmented horizontally (in relation to the different national ministries and agencies dealing with the nation brand with responsibility for tourism communication and promotion, investment promotion and export promotion) and vertically (in relation to roles and competences of the central government and the regional governments concerning economic development and tourism). The many organizations dealing with the nation brand are not an issue per se, but this certainly implies the need for significant efforts in terms of coordination and leadership. Another reason might be the relatively weak 'place branding culture' in the country where at local, regional and national levels, a degree of reluctance to integrate a proper branding approach into place marketing strategies (beyond the design of logos and slogans) is fairly evident.

Internal branding – in contrast with the nation brand internationalization – has not firmly entered the lively national debate on the Italy brand. Corroborating the internal negative sentiment mentioned previously, studies confirmed a 'perceptual distortion' amongst Italians who believe the country has more crime, poverty, migration, unemployment and economic marginality than is actually the case (Rebotti, 2019). This suggests the underestimation of the importance of leveraging the nation brand to thicken the internal relationscape (i.e. the set of relations that, more or less active and visible, influence actions) and the relevance of rooting the nation brand in it (Pasquinelli, 2017).

2.1 Brand Italy for FDI promotion

The ITA-Italian Trade Agency is the national agency through which the central government promotes economic development and supports national firms in international markets. ITA-Invest in Italy is the division in charge of promoting and facilitating foreign direct investments into the country. In the field of investment promotion, Invitalia is another national agency providing assistance and services to investors.

Place branding has been marginal in FDI promotion, with the functional approach to marketing prevailing over the representational one (Pasquinelli and Vuignier, 2019). In the Italian context, marketing actions have consisted in the activation of FDI offices in various countries, the participation in international fairs and events to inform audiences about investment opportunities in the country, the *Invest in Italy* web page providing information about key contacts, opportunities and success stories. A dedicated website to real estate was launched (www.investinitalyrealestate.com), a database of public real estate that is open for investments, including the Italian state properties.

ITA-Italian Trade Agency has defined various agreements with regional governments to coordinate investment promotion strategies: some regions have been particularly active in FDI promotion, such as Lombardy and Tuscany.

2.2 Brand Italy for export: 'Made in Italy'

The ITA-Italian Trade Agency is in charge of the 'Made in Italy' promotion. The 2020 marketing plan allocated about 22 million euros including 23% of private funds and included actions such as the participation in fairs and events (40% total budget), training, actions addressing distribution channels, communication, surveys and sectoral analyses. The top five geographical markets for budget expenditure were the United States, Germany, Japan, China and the Emirates (in this order). In terms of sectors, agri-food is the main sector of investments (38%), followed by electronic machinery and equipment (34%), and fashion and lifestyle (14%).

Over recent years, marketing and communication campaigns focused on 'Made in Italy' with different sectoral and geographic scopes. Table 5.1 provides some examples. Much attention has been drawn to the agri-food sectors which have become central to 'Made in Italy': Expo Milano 2015 boosted this central role, focusing on the theme of *Feeding the Planet, Energy for Life* and raising interest for agricultural policy, food security, nutrition and well-being from a sustainability and territorial development perspective. The *True Italian Taste* project maintains the Expo legacy, as the identified core brand associations (see Table 5.1) suggest.

The 2015 Expo was an opportunity for nation branding and the *Italy the Extraordinary Commonplace* campaign aimed to expand the nation brand knowledge, levering yet going beyond Italian stereotypes (e.g. Latin lovers, mommy's boys, party addicts, incurable idlers, gesticulators, crazy drivers, eternal children, *dolce vita* lovers, food enthusiasts, football maniacs), to trigger associations with innovation, science, research and engineering, which tend to remain marginal in the nation brand image. In this campaign, history and tradition, art and cultural heritage were confirmed at the core of the nation brand, as well as the Italian lifestyle, represented as a constant and passionate search for quality and excellence.

Beyond sectoral initiatives, *helloITA* is the 'Italian national brand hub' providing Italian brands from diverse sectors with a common window on the Alibaba platform, which targets the Chinese market. On this e-commerce platform 'Made in Italy' brands are represented under the same national umbrella which aims to give Italian firms visibility, provide coherent knowledge about 'Made in Italy' and educate consumers. This virtual commercial hub not only is in charge of supporting excellent Italian products but it also aims to boost awareness and knowledge about Italian culture, traditions and craftsmanship.[1] In 2019 the *We Are Together* campaign was launched in the context of *helloITA* and consisted of the design of online and offline channel initiatives to diffuse 'Made in Italy' in the Chinese market and cities, with special attention to Chinese millennials.

Table 5.1 'Made in Italy': examples of marketing and communication campaigns

Name of the campaign	Launch year	Sector(s)	Promotor(s)/ Partner(s)	Target market	Core brand associations
Italy the Extraordinary Commonplace	2015 (Expo Milano 2015)	Various sectors: infrastructure, jewellery, manufactured goods, machinery, furniture, automotive, pharmaceutical– biomedical products, aerospace technologies	Ministry of Economic Development/ITA-Italian Trade Agency	Worldwide	Engineering Technology R&D Science Heritage
Extraordinary Italian Taste 'Buy authentic Italian, get more'	2015	Agri-food	ITA for MISE/Ministry of Economic Development	North America	Quality Italian know-how Variety and diversity of ingredients and food products Historical tradition
True Italian Taste (part of Extraordinary Italian Taste)	2017	Agri-food	Ministry of Foreign Affairs and International Cooperation (in charge of international trade since 1st January 2020)/ International Italian Chambers of Commerce	North and South America, Europe, Asia, Australia	100% Made in Italy Nutrition and health Link with territories Quality ingredients Innovative food: recipes, distribution, packaging Culinary art

(*Continued*)

Table 5.1 (Continued)

Name of the campaign	Launch year	Sector(s)	Promotor(s)/ Partner(s)	Target market	Core brand associations
Italian wine – Taste the passion	2018	Wine	ITA-Italian Trade Agency	Worldwide	Passion for the Italian lifestyle/ Taste of living Excellence History of wine production Style Art and Opera music Contemporary architecture Diversity
helloITA 'We Are Together' (multichannel campaign)	2018 2019	Various sectors (100 Italian brands under the same umbrella on Alibaba): fashion, food and wine, lifestyle	ITA-Italian Trade Agency/ Alibaba	China	Italian taste and culture Share and follow your passion Technology Tradition and craft Excellence

Source: Author's own elaboration

2.3 *Brand Italy for tourism*

ENIT is the Italian National Tourist Board in charge of 'promoting the unified image of the Italian tourist offer'. ENIT promotes Italy as a destination in international tourism markets and also through the web portal *italia.it*. A crucial point characterizing Italian tourism governance is that by constitutional law the regional governments are competent for tourism promotion: regions are fairly proactive in marketing their tourism offering and invest in regional branding, not without raising concerns about the risks of an international positioning outside of the strong frame of the Italy brand. A referendum in 2016 proposed a review of the Constitution which, amongst the various implications, would have drawn tourism competences to the central government. The referendum was, however, unsuccessful.

The National Tourism Strategic Plan 2017–2022 designed by the Ministry for Cultural Assets and Tourism identified the strengthening of the nation brand, beyond any fragmentation, as a key objective of effective and innovative marketing. The actions to pursue this objective include (a) unitary promotion and image coordination in favour of the nation brand; (b) integrated promotion with 'Made in Italy'; (c) immaterial cultural heritage promotion; (d) harmonization of regional marketing plans through the definition of interregional projects. Integration is, thus, pursued from a twofold perspective, which means an integration of the nation brand across regional actions and an integration across the different brand functions, drawing a strong link between tourism and 'Made in Italy' (export). The linkage is two-sided: 'Made in Italy' represents a distinctive factor of international competitiveness for the country, influencing international tourism markets; on the other hand, tourism provides a cultural experiential platform for 'Made in Italy' products (Bellini and Pasquinelli, 2016).

The ENIT marketing plan 2019–2022 includes branding actions motivated by the need for the nation brand 'to get through deep change'. The national tourism board's task is to catalyse private and public actors' actions towards a homogenization of local promotion initiatives, in order to provide the nation brand with strong and coherent positioning. Particular emphasis has been on establishing partnerships with 'Made in Italy' brands to strengthen the nation brand.[2]

3. Brand Italy in the COVID-19 crisis: towards a nation-branding strategy?

The COVID-19 pandemic outbreak found the Italian system in a phase of growing and widespread awareness about the need to invest in the nation brand more strategically, to untap its potential of an umbrella brand supporting city and region brands as well as the different national economic realities. Beyond the statements emerging in business, political and academic contexts, the design of a nation branding strategy, the approach to branding, the brand development process and the brand governance configuration, capable of innovating, managing and maintaining the nation brand, have not clearly emerged yet. Relevant but still fairly fragmented and partial actions have been put in place in absence of a comprehensive branding framework.

The COVID-19 crisis seems to have accelerated the transition towards a nation-branding strategy. The significant impact of the COVID-19 crisis on the tourism industry and on exports reinvigorated the debate on national competitiveness and boosted the idea that the country brand has to be seriously considered as crucial leverage to enhance Italy's competitiveness. The country brand has become fairly central in the mediatic discourse on the national economic recovery.

The Ministry of Foreign Affairs and International Cooperation (from 1st January 2020 in charge of international trade and the country's internationalization, with a focus on 'the country system promotion'), in partnership with ITA – Italian Trade Agency and AgID (Agency for Digital Italy), recently launched a 'Made in Italy' programme that includes a communication campaign. Designed to respond to the COVID-19 crisis in the agri-food business, confirmed as central to 'Made in Italy,' and in the other severely impacted sectors, this campaign has the ambition to relaunch the country image 'through a nation branding campaign' and to sustain export performance. This initiative will look for 'promotional synergies' by exploring opportunities for intersectoral and integrated approaches across 'useful adjacencies' and production chains such as tourism, hospitality, craftmanship, UNESCO sites and various other sectors.[3]

A market consultation was launched in June 2020 through public meetings gathering interest and ideas about innovative methodologies and tools in order to design competitive calls for tenders for communication campaigns in support of export and internationalization of the national economic system. A total investment of 50 million euros was allocated. As the general director of ITA-Italian Trade Agency put it, 'for many years we felt the need of a nation branding campaign . . . today the time has come'.[4]

It is not possible to state if this initiative will be effective in sustaining the nation brand through a robust, long-lasting and integrated strategy (multisectoral and multi-level, i.e. national, regional, local levels). Certainly, beyond innovation and creativity in the modalities to channel the brand into international markets, innovation and creativity will be central to outline the core brand associations that, rooted in national heritage, have to mirror the country and its community nowadays. In this regard, internal branding approaches and techniques should not be overlooked.

The COVID-19 crisis and the response of the country to the emergency and lockdown, for instance, seem to have renewed some national values and made them visible worldwide. International media extensively commented the 'Everything will be all right' message and children's rainbow drawings out of home windows, as well as Italians singing the anthem and other traditional songs from their balconies in several Italian cities. This was interpreted as a unique and 'creative' reaction to the harsh lockdown, a way 'to feel a community, and to participate in the collective grief' ('Italians find a moment of joy in this moment of anxiety,' the *New York Times*, 14 March 2020). Recent surveys showed that amongst Italians the level of trust in the National Sanitary System grew significantly during the emergency (for 89% of respondents), and a solidarity attitude increased with a rising propensity to donate (BVA Doxa, 2020).

One key challenge for nation branding is the integration of emerging and 'lived' values internally engaging the national community, with the consolidated storytelling of 'Bel Paese' (beautiful country), 'bello e ben fatto' (beautiful and well done) and 'dolce vita' (the sweet life), which has shown significant and long-lasting international appeal. Would such integration contribute to a more competitive nation brand? What can this tell about the contemporary nation to international audiences potentially interested in travelling, buying quality goods and services, investing, working and studying in the country? What would it say to domestic audiences? Another crucial challenge consists in the definition of governance and processes that make the rejuvenation and strengthening of Italy's symbolic infrastructure realistic and viable.

Notes

1 www.ice.it/it/node/5392 last access 28 July 2020.
2 www.enit.it/wwwenit/it/pressroomonline/comunicati-stampa/3136-enit-piano-triennale-centinaio-palmucci.html, last access 29 July 2020.
3 https://appaltinnovativi.gov.it/made-in-italy last access 29 July 2020.
4 https://drive.google.com/file/d/1PI1_hhgRe9voBD-yCI_amo2kpdTxB_Jz/view last access 29 July 2020.

References

Aaker, D. A., and Joachimsthaler, E. (2000) The Brand Relationship Spectrum: The Key to the Brand Architecture Challenge. *California Management Review*, 42(2), 8–23.

Bellini, N., and Pasquinelli, C. (2016) Urban Brandscape as Value Ecosystem: The Cultural Destination Strategy of Fashion Brands. *Journal of Place Branding and Public Diplomacy*, 12, 5–16.

BVA Doxa. (2019) *Percezione, atteggiamenti e abitudini: gli italiani all'epoca del Covid-19.* www.bva-doxa.com/percezione-atteggiamenti-e-abitudini-gli-italiani-allepoca-del-covid-19/, accessed July 29, 2020.

FutureBrand. (2019) *FutureBrand Country Index 2019.* Retrieved from https://www.futurebrand.com/futurebrand-country-index.

Napolitano, M. R., and De Nisco, A. (2017) Cultural Heritage: The Missing "Link" in the Place Marketing Literature Chain. *Journal of Place Branding and Public Diplomacy*, 13, 101–106.

Pasquinelli, C. (2017) *Place branding. Percezione, illusione e concretezza.* Aracne, Roma.

Pasquinelli, C., and Vuignier, R. (2019) Place Marketing, Policy Integration and Governance Complexity: An Analytical Framework for FDI Promotion. *European Planning Studies*, 28(7), 1413–1430.

Rebotti, M. (2019) Il primato degli italiani nel regno delle percezioni errate. *Corriere della Sera*, 13 May.

Symbola. (2017) *Be-Italy. Indagine sull'attrattività del Paese.* Fondazione per le Qualità Italiane Symbola.

6 Spain

Gildo Seisdedos

Introduction

Branding Spain is a challenging task. At a supra-regional level, it shares the ingredient branding coexistence of the country's brand with the territorial umbrella brand of the EU, a challenge shared with all the other EU countries. But within the country itself is where we can find an additional, particular point of complexity that stems from the coexistence of two kinds of regional entities. On the one hand, we find those which can be merely considered 'regions'. On the other hand, in others, we see more or less robust aspirations to become an individual state due to the relevance of nationalist, independence-oriented political movements. The Spanish Constitution recognizes a specific process of territorial decentralization for these so-called historic regions: initially Galicia, Catalonia and the Basque Country but also followed by Navarre. This duality explains why the Spanish Constitution introduced the hazy category of 'autonomous communities' to encompass both realities, thus avoiding hurting political sensitiveness. This context makes, in these two cases, the role of regional branding quite different; being also a source of discrepancy and conflict and adding complexity to brand governance.

An additional fact to consider when branding Spain is the relevance of tourism within the national economy. Accounting for more than 12% of GDP before the COVID-19 crisis, Spain's branding has been highly influenced by tourists as the primary stakeholders and target audience of its country branding efforts.

In short, Spain, as a country brand, is a politically -multifaceted, touristic-at-heart brand. These two traits strongly condition its governance and define its idiosyncrasy when compared to other countries.

Brand management

As we can deduce from the previous paragraphs, answering who is in charge of the brand Spain is a challenging question. Country brand governance is

DOI: 10.4324/9781003084051-6

always a touchy, political issue where conflict is likely to arise. Managing these disputes involves either a clear-cut hierarchical competence distribution or well-defined cooperation; neither of those is the general rule in the Spanish case.

We could describe how this is managed following two criteria: territorial level (national, regional or local) and target markets (tourism, investment) even if they are both deeply interwoven.

At a national, state-scale level, there is a traditional tension between two government ministries (the Ministry of Industry, Trade and Tourism and the Ministry of Foreign Affairs) competing to be responsible for managing Spain's brand.

The latter follows a public diplomacy approach claiming that this topic falls within their competences. Competences ranging from the traditional network of embassies updated with more recent ideas of soft power, based on the use of economic and cultural influence managed by Cultural or Economic) Attachés. The Instituto Cervantes is probably the most relevant example of these policies articulated around the Spanish language with 87 centres in 44 countries.

The Ministry of Industry, Trade and Tourism is leading initiatives oriented towards opening new markets for Spanish companies leveraging on Spain as an umbrella brand.

There is a clear consensus that the relevance and dimension of the challenge requires direct reporting to the Prime Minister. But government silos are hard to break: initially created as High Commissioner for Brand Spain (2012), this governmental body has been, since 2018, part of the Ministry of Foreign Affairs.

As a result of these constraints (with an evident political background), the promotion of Spain as a brand is weak, lacks a bold positioning, and is confined to a diplomatic, technocratic environment.

At a regional level, autonomous communities have followed very different paths which we can simplify into a common trait for all and two alternative roadmaps.

The common thread would be the delegation of tourism promotion from the state to the regions. This fact has led to a wide variety of promotional efforts, conveying many different messages to a myriad of potential visitors. This is arguably a good approach as one of the main assets of Spain as a tourism destination is the diversity of regions with strong personalities. Potential visitors cannot say they know Spain having visited just one region, as Spain encompasses many different and diverse local and regional sub-destinations.

In Spain, the Ministry of Industry is also the Ministry of Trade and Tourism. This makes sense in a country with such an overwhelming focus on tourism, which could be considered to be the country's leading industry. This ministry plays a supportive, coordination role for regional governments, but the latter enjoy almost complete autonomy in this field.

Concerning differences between autonomous communities, two patterns emerge. Some of these communities focus their branding efforts on tourism promotion. But others have added to this tourist agenda a small-scale replica (or embryo) of the public diplomacy of a country-state. This extension has created conflict. Can a region create its network of embassies? The Basque Country has deployed a network of 'commercial embassies' while Catalonia has developed a network of 'international delegations'.

Finally, at a local level, the main cities in Spain have also replicated the policies of their regions developing tourism (and economic development) departments. These local bodies share the same goals as their regional counterparts.

Governance model assessment

This governance model, like such models, has strengths and weaknesses.

On the plus side, we could say this model has generated, mainly regarding tourism, positive internal competition that helps to foster efficiency and diversity. On the same note, emphasizing differences has developed attractive destinations for a more significant number of target markets, allowing a greater market reach. One can find specific destinations for almost every nationality, budget or leisure profile. Achieving this successfully from a more centralized model would probably have been impossible.

On the negative side, in a globalized world, applying this model to business attraction is not as efficient; companies are averse to this complexity as it implies legal uncertainty when confronting a sea of local regulations. Additionally, for both cases, no doubt resources are in many cases wasted due to redundancy as two (or even three) administrations are spending money for the same goal, thereby losing focus and also losing out on the evident advantages of economies of scale.

Brand value proposition and architecture: diagnosis, challenges and the road ahead

The brand Spain is a highly recognized brand, associated with a set of positive values that Miro's sun still reflects today. The principal value proposition is quality of life: an attractive lifestyle with an optimal balance between tradition and modernity.

This nucleus has two main dimensions. The first dimension is *fiesta* and *siesta* (both, not by chance, globalized Spanish words). It is the most ludic part, encompassing nightlife, leisure, joie de vivre, weather, coast and sea and food. The second dimension is artistic genius and creativity linking cultural heritage to a set of contemporary world-class architects, artists, chefs, sportspeople and so on.

Both dimensions are clearly depicted on Miro's sun: Spain is sun and beach but qualified with a high-quality, genuine cultural offer ranging from flamenco to popular celebrations on a safe, European-quality-standard environment. This positioning makes Spain, essentially, a touristic brand at heart. A very successful touristic brand as all pre-COVID indicators clearly show.

Nevertheless, the main challenge for brand Spain is evolving this brand from a purely touristic one to a new positioning that, resting on these strengths, also reflects the economic dimension of the country. The brand Spain needs to reflect not only a significant touristic power but also a dynamic and creative economy.

Consequently, the greatest weakness of the brand Spain is being perceived just as a 'sun and beach' destination with a strong personality, cultural sophistication and high-quality public services and infrastructures but not as a real economic developed power. Spain ranks 13th in nominal GDP (IMF, 2020)[1] just ahead of the Netherlands, Australia and Mexico, countries that already enjoy this economic dimension as part of their brands.

Bringing in this dimension to the brand Spain is its most vital and urgent challenge. But how to do it? Taking advantage of Spanish brands as brand ambassadors of the brand Spain is a fascinating field not well enough explored. Good proof of it is that the use of their Spanish origin is scarce amongst Spanish brands (compare, for instance, Zara and Burberry). Exploring public–private partnerships to associate the brand Spain with the communication of leading Spanish brands seems a feasible, cheap and efficient tool to make the brand Spain evolve towards more competitive positioning.

On that particular note, we can highlight the role of the Leading Brands of Spain Forum, an initiative of leading Spanish brands to highlight the importance of brands for the companies and for the Spanish economy, building a public–private strategic alliance, and increasing awareness about the importance of the role of Spain as a brand for internationalization. More than 110 associates contribute, alongside the government bodies and with the support of key players in civil society (such as its 60 Spain brand honorary ambassadors) to strengthen the prestige associated with the international image of Spain.

European Union and Spanish brand portfolio: cobranding without frictions

We have already described the frictions, redundancies and lack of coordination between national and regional territorial layers in Spain regarding brand management. Paradoxically, this competition and mistrust disappears when European and Spanish (any level) policymakers interact.

The European Union is regarded as a brand that adds positive value to the Spanish brand. That could be explained by years of EU funding to update Spanish infrastructure as well as for the embedded values of modernity, democracy and stability of the EU brand. Year after year, Spain leads the list of countries more identified with Europe, well above the European average.

Another example of this peaceful, synergic coexistence is that the previously described historic autonomous communities compete with the state for policies but, at the same time, emphasize that their aspirations for greater self-government are compatible with belonging to the EU.

Conclusions

- The brand Spain encompasses a complex brand architecture with a variable geometry where not all regions have the same aspirations regarding brand governance. Managing this brand ecosystem requires coordination mechanisms or clear-cut hierarchical competence distribution, but in many cases there are conflicting approaches.
- As a tourism destination, Spain is a polycentric, rich brand with strong awareness and very positive associations. In this field, the previously described governance model has added richness and nuances, enhancing the attractiveness of Spain as a myriad of diverse destinations, well communicated by regional policymakers but enjoying the synergies of Spain as an umbrella brand.
- The balance is not so positive when the brand Spain addresses investors and global consumers to sell economic attractiveness, such as the appeal of made-in-Spain products. The touristic brand eclipses this dimension and the diffuse governance model becomes inefficient in conveying the image (rooted in reality) of a dynamic economic environment hosting world-class, highly competitive companies.

Cobranding with the EU brand is actively sought by national and regional policymakers as Europeanism is a value deeply rooted in Spain.

Note

1 IMF (2020): World Economic Outlook, A Long and Difficult Ascent, International Monetary Fund, October 2020.

7   Russia

Kirill Rozhkov

Introduction

Over the past decade and a half the anti-globalization movement fuelled by the world economic crisis has resulted in significant shifts in the world political system – the growth of nationalism, return of trade and migration barriers between countries, introduction of numerous sanctions, and so on. The 'hard' factors of competition between countries started to replace the 'soft' ones, such as concern for international image and reputation.

Russia has also become involved in these processes. Since 2014, it has been subject to economic and political sanctions, to which it has often responded reciprocally.

Economically, this has inevitably led to a decrease in the country's integration into the world economy: a decline in international capital flows (both inbound and outbound), import substitution, and a decline in real incomes and consumption.

As a result, there have been significantly fewer efforts to attract world resources to contribute to the country's development. Particularly, the interest in attracting FDI has decreased significantly following the sanctions, so there are limited efforts to attract foreign investments.

The devaluation of the rouble in the mid-2010s did not cause a significant rise in inbound tourist arrivals, but at the same time it fostered the development of domestic tourism. The pandemic in 2019–2020 has caused a disruption of international tourism, including inbound tourist flows to Russia, which has increased the role of domestic tourism. Hence, the relative importance of long-term improvement of the country's attractiveness for internal tourists has also increased.

At the same time, there can be seen more efforts to enhance the image of Russia for the Russians themselves by appealing to patriotism and national identity in domestic politics, mass media, culture and education. This creates conditions for the formation of a specific profile of the nation brand.

DOI: 10.4324/9781003084051-7

This article describes the process and results of creating the nation brand of Russia.

Conceptual framework

There are two conceptual starting points for nation branding. The first one is the pragmatic desire to gain social and economic resources belonging to external and internal audiences. To achieve that goal, one has to create an image that would be attractive for those audiences and meet their expectations. The distinctive features of that image are closely connected with marketing goals. This approach is based on the philosophy of social constructivism.

The second starting point is the complete opposite of this. Using economic and social advantages from cooperation with other nations is a secondary (not primary) goal for the nation. The primary goal is to retain and reinforce national identity as the key condition for development of the nation (i.e. methodological nationalism). Therefore, the distinctive features of the created image are closely connected with what a nation (but not target audiences) values and thinks about itself. At the same time, according to this view, the nation itself and its external environment must accept it as it is and all relationships with the nation must be based on this.

Which concept will turn out to be more relevant for a particular nation depends on what its society values most at any particular stage of its development – either economic advantages or national pride and identity.

A nation image includes different components that can be formed separately as well as in certain connections with one another. In this chapter, fully fledged nation brand management is considered to take place if the following features are present when creating a nation image:

1   stakeholders that are involved in the promotion of the nation image
2   targets achieved by stakeholders while promoting the nation image
3   value propositions of the nation
4   projects that promote the nation image
5   non-administrative and non-financial tools for attracting the attention and resources of target audiences
6   touchpoints of the target audiences with the nation image
7   impact of the promoted nation image evidenced by the behaviour of the target audiences (family, business/work, studies, recreation and travel)
8   involving a significant number of foreign citizens in realization of the projects (see item 4)
9   using architecture and an urban environment as communication channels of the image.

If the above set of features is not complete, we can speak about underbrand, that is, an image that is at some stage of evolution into a brand.

In this analysis, a stakeholder is an organization or individual that is a resident of the country and:

- communicates with target audiences within the country and abroad
- uses the names 'Russia' and/or 'Russian' in their communications

The stakeholder's goal can be to create stable associations with the country, that is, their efforts can be intentionally and directly aimed at forming the country image.

The stakeholders are also people and organizations that use the country's name and symbols in order to achieve their own goals. The way they do this also affects the nation image, though indirectly and sometimes unintentionally.

The main part of this chapter describes the seven key components of the image of Russia that have been formed or are in the process of active formation at the time of writing. In this analysis, an image is considered to be a key one if it is widely publicized in the media, transmitted by stakeholders and discussed.

Two of the seven key components of the image of Russia are analysed in detail, whereas the remaining five are described in the more limited terms of their value propositions, stakeholders and main projects.

Based on the comparison of the evolution level of the image components and the degree of their interrelationship, conclusions are drawn about the essence and current state of the nation brand of Russia, as well as the prospects for its further development.

Country which defeated fascism

Value proposition: a way of life and ideology that are incompatible with those of fascism.

The image component is aimed at preserving the nation's common historical memory and uniting people (also with the government), as well as at protecting the truth about World War II, not in the geopolitical context but in the historical context (historical justice).

A great number of stakeholders are involved in the formation of this component – governmental institutions and those public organizations affiliated with the government that actively cooperate within the following projects that are united around patriotism:

- the main national holiday Victory Day (President, federal government and parliament) celebrated annually with a military parade (Ministry of Defence)

- history curriculum (Ministry of Education)
- cultural policy (production of war and historical films by the Ministry of Culture)
- military history festivals and archaeological excavations in the battlegrounds by the Russian Military Historical Society, patriotic education of youth and special projects of the Ministry of Defence)
- erecting monuments in honour of the fallen (city authorities) with the help of both state funds and public donations

The image component is supported by the international mass movement 'Immortal Regiment,' that can be viewed as a focal stakeholder of the image component. The *country which defeated fascism* image component corresponds to the full-fledged nation brand since the image component possesses the complete set of brand features outlined earlier. By cooperating with the authorities, the movement gained access to huge media and administrative resources, quickly expanded its geography and engaged the entire Russian society and a large part of the world community.

The movement has no analogues in Russia in terms of scale of events that are held annually in all regions of Russia. The Immortal Regiment processions attract unprecedented numbers of participants. For example, on 9 May 2019 more than 1 million people took part in the procession in Saint Petersburg. By May 2019, the descendants of war veterans and home front workers have created almost 440,000 family histories on the movement website. This includes the stories of those who fought on the fronts of the Great Patriotic War and behind enemy lines, as well as home front workers, concentration camp prisoners, and war children. In 2015, the Immortal Regiment marched through 1,150 cities and towns located in 17 countries of the world. By 2020, the Immortal Regiment movement had spread to 80 countries and territories.

The *country which defeated fascism* image component is conceptually connected with (and derived from) the *Mysterious Russian soul* image component. Russian history shows the intolerance of Russians to any occupation and willingness to unite in order to fight against a common enemy, forgetting about any contradictions within society.

By joining the project, the government has gained the support of society in an important topic for the people as well as the opportunity to use this support in promoting other nation image components, first of all, the *Fair World Power* component.

However, the connection of this key component of the image of Russia with other key components is rather weak.

Culture of world significance

The image of the country possessing a unique culture of world significance/ world cultural heritage is heterogeneous. As a rule, it is formed by projects that are weakly connected to one another and reflect different (in terms of the cultural process) value propositions as well as differences in the stakeholders' interests.

Cultural heritage located in Moscow and Saint Petersburg makes both cities the largest generators of inbound tourist arrivals. With projects such as Mausoleum, Perestroika and Gorbachev, 'Perm – European Capital of Culture,' Sochi Winter Olympics, and the restoration of constructivist buildings, Russia is also promoted as a social experimenter and the birthplace of the avant-garde.

However, a significant part of Russia's cultural heritage is actively promoted only domestically market but is little-known abroad. For example, the umbrella tourist project 'The Golden Ring of Russia' unites ancient Russian cities (founded from the 11th to 17th centuries). Now the project involves many regional governments, businesses and NGOs, while the itinerary attracts 8 million tourists annually. The Golden Ring has inspired others to emulate its success by creating similar umbrella brands.

In the late 20th and early 21st century a new movement in the branding of Russian towns appeared on the base of deliberately invented images that do however have certain historical foundations, such as legends about real historical figures or even images of fairy-tale characters. Examples of this include the 'Mouse Museum' in Myshkin, Yaroslavl and the 'Homeland of Father Frost' in Veliky Ustyug, Vologda. The concepts of this and similar projects have added their own mythological subcomponent to the cultural component of the nation image of Russia. Souvenirs for foreign tourists, vodka, matryoshkas, bears and balalaika represent to a very limited extent only the external side of this subcomponent.

With some exceptions, a special feature of the *Culture of world significance* nation image component is a large number of stakeholders with relatively limited organizational, media and financial resources. Resource scarcity is compensated for by creativity in generating various value propositions and tools for image creation and management as well as wide participation of benefactors and volunteers.

However, none of the subcomponents of the cultural component of image of Russia has a full set of features of nation brand management – they are all underbranded:

- classical culture brands that promote Russia abroad do not have a wide audience at home
- avant-garde is promoted by relatively influential stakeholders, projects and approaches, but it has mixed perceptions in conservative regions

and among local communities, and that is why it has not become part of the nation's everyday life

- mythological culture has greater significance for Russians than classical and avant-garde culture, but the former is much less known abroad. However, most often the efforts to commercialize the mythological culture are not enough even to attract domestic tourists due to the lack of relevant competence and skills among local authorities

At the same time, however, the key nation image component is closely connected with most of the other components in that it:

- is the embodiment of 'soft power' in international relations, which allows Russia to consider itself and be perceived as part of Europe (the '*European Dream of Peter the Great*' component);
- augments the Orthodox culture (the '*Moscow, Third Rome*' component) with a secular one and through museum activities contributes to the preservation of antiquities that belonged to the Russian Orthodox Church;
- is significantly reinforced by the '*Fair World Power*' component, primarily through the use of the Russian language in the post-Soviet states;
- is especially strongly linked to the '*Mysterious Russian Soul*' component with creativity being one of its attributes.

This allows us to conclude that the cultural component of nation image of Russia has great prospects of becoming a nation brand, provided that the missing elements of brand management will be developed. The other components of Russia's nation image are summarized in the following sections.

European dream of Peter the Great

Value propositions: realization of the idea of a city which is perfect from the point of view of architecture, urban planning and city community.

Stakeholders: community of Saint-Petersburg, President of Russia, Gazprom Corporation.

Projects: development of the city of Saint-Petersburg.

Mysterious Russian soul

Value propositions: a specific form of feeling free in Russia.

Projects: celebration of Yuri Gagarin, 2018 FIFA World Cup, the transformation of state-owned plots of land into dachas, Masha and the Bear animated series, and so on.

The main weakness of the component is that, though being connected with almost all other components of the nation image, it is dissolved in the culture and everyday life of Russians and is not institutionalized.

Fair world power

Value propositions:

- the idea of a multipolar world and the promise of justice in international relations;
- the largest territory and richest natural resources in the world;
- the promise of protecting national interests protection.

Stakeholders: President of Russia, Ministry of Foreign Affairs, Ministry of Defense, Russian Geographical Society.

Projects/topics: Russian humanitarian missions worldwide, Crimea's reunification with Russia, support for the Donbass, military operations in South Ossetia, Abkhazia, Syria, patriotic education of youth, protection of wildlife, promotion of alternative tourism in Russia, Trans-Siberian Railway tours.

Moscow, Third Rome

Value proposition: Orthodox Church values and a state ideology based on them, the concept of the Russian Orthodox Church as a successor of the Byzantine Empire.

Stakeholders: Russian Orthodox Church, President of Russia, Ministry of Culture, Ministry of Education, Ministry of Defense.

Projects/topics: returning of church property to its owners, the programme for building new churches in Moscow, erecting monuments to Orthodox saints, religious studies in the school curriculum, construction of the Main Cathedral of the Russian Armed Forces, 'Meshchovsk – Birthplace of Two Tsarinas.'

Birthplace of talents/brains

Value proposition: a way of life and social circumstances producing creative people.

Stakeholders: President of Russia, Skolkovo Foundation, leading universities, state industrial associations (Russian Export Centre, etc.), business associations (Chamber of Commerce and Industry), Ministry of Science and Higher Education, Ministry of Economic Development.

Projects/topics: Russians Nobel Prize winners, space (International Space Station), Kalashnikov and weapons exports, 'Made in Russia,' national quality monitoring system 'Roskachestvo'.

In this image component there is a lack of systematic management: there are several stakeholders that are responsible for promoting the component internationally, but they do not coordinate their efforts.

Conclusions

Most of the nation image components that have sufficient resources at their disposal and which enjoy stakeholder support both in the country and abroad are aimed at Russians themselves (*Country which defeated fascism, Fair world power, Moscow, Third Rome*). The only image component that is actively developed both domestically and internationally is the *European Dream of Peter the Great*.

The following conclusions can also be made:

- there are multiple entities sending communications about Russia's nation brand
- not all of the communication messages are created and sent with the use of a clear strategy and implementation and control procedures, or are supported by the general public
- not all of these entities collaborate and coordinate their efforts, which is why internal audiences often receive a whole range of weakly connected nation image components rather than one single and agreed image.

The image components that were found to have the biggest number of connections with the other ones are '*Culture of World Significance*' and '*Mysterious Russian Soul*'.

These image components also have the most manifestations in the everyday life and consciousness of Russians.

However, both of these image components suffer from a lack of resources, proposition diversity, and limited interaction between stakeholders. Provided that the gaps in management are bridged, these two images have the greatest potential to become part of the nation brand of Russia in the foreseeable future.

In conclusion, it can be argued that there is no single and consistent image of Russia communicated through the media. The country is very heterogeneous both regionally and socially, which is why there is rarely a common understanding of what Russia is and should be among the different entities involved in communicating the Russian brand.

In light of this, we can state that there is no consistent nation branding strategy in Russia at the moment.

8 Sweden

Marcus Andersson

Introduction

The purpose of this chapter is to describe Sweden's approach to nation branding and outline lessons learned from the work.

Management and strategy

On the highest strategic level, the brand is governed by the Board for Promoting Sweden Abroad. Created in 1996, it is an inter-agency and inter-ministerial board reporting to the Ministry of Foreign Affairs (MFA) and with the MFA, Ministry of Enterprise, Ministry of Culture, Swedish Institute, Visit Sweden and Business Sweden as members. The Board's regular members are Director Generals and CEOs of the government agencies and Head of Units at the three ministries. It is chaired by the MFA and currently sits under the Minister for Foreign Trade and Nordic Affairs. The Board typically meets four times a year to decide about strategic direction and budgets.

Two additional layers of coordinating groups are part of the Board's governance and management of the brand. A group comprising Heads of Communication at the ministries and department heads at the government agencies meet to coordinate and align specific communication and promotion efforts. On the operational level, working groups with project managers, analysts and strategists as members gather to discuss and agree on issues that pertain to implementation. At the time of writing, two such groups are active: one on visual identity and one on analysis of the brand image. These groups meet two to three times in a quarter.

All the promotion work is guided by a strategy – Strategy for the Promotion of Sweden Abroad – that came into effect in 2013. It was preceded by a communications and branding platform comprising a positioning and four core values (read more about these in the next section). The platform was

DOI: 10.4324/9781003084051-8

adopted after 3 years of research and consultations. The strategy and the brand platform have been modified and adapted, but the core of the platform and strategy has been consistent since 2007 and 2013 respectively. Interestingly, neither the platform nor the strategy has changed following national elections and new governments coming into power.

Out of the ministries and government agencies that make up the Board for Promoting Sweden Abroad, two government agencies are particularly active in the management and implementation of the brand strategy: the Swedish Institute and Visit Sweden.

The brand value proposition

The strategy is based on the idea that cross-border cooperation is essential for tackling the global challenges of the future. The main theme is that Sweden's free and open society should function as a hub for innovation and co-creation that can address major challenges in the world – and the communication and marketing aim to build an image of a progressive country that strives to identify and create future-oriented solutions.

The strategy rests on four main pillars:

1   Vision of the future – 'We see a world where innovation and cocreation are important for tackling major challenges'
2   Objective – Sweden's free and open society is a hub for innovation and co-creation
3   Purpose – To promote trade, attract investment, tourists and talent, and encourage cultural exchange
4   Core values – Innovative, Open, Authentic, Caring

Having been part of the strategy since its creation, the four core values of the brand platform of the strategy are meant to permeate all promotion efforts. A fifth, overarching core value – progressive – was part of the brand platform for a long time.

Main areas promoted

With a view to creating the conditions for a sharper focus and greater impact in promoting the image of the country, four profile areas have been identified. These are society, innovation, creativity and sustainability. The positioning is supported by a number of indices that rank Sweden at the top, in factors such as sustainability, innovation and equality.

The profile area *society* is promoted by stressing Sweden's focus on human rights and equal opportunities, which in combination with entrepreneurship and conscious reform efforts have resulted in a social model that has attracted interest abroad. *Innovation* is promoted by referring to the fact that Sweden is continuously ranked as one of the most innovative countries in the word, and by focusing on business promotion and investment and talent attraction, as well as highlighting Swedish successes in the area of innovation. *Sustainability* focuses on ecological sustainability, the environment and climate. It is promoted by emphasizing that the country has a long tradition of international commitment to supporting active global cooperation on sustainable development. Finally, *creativity* is about communicating that Sweden is a significant actor in the cultural and creative industries. This profile area is also meant to help creating a modern image of the country as an imaginative and innovative country.

There is an intention to adapt the profile areas to the context and current situation in a particular location or market.

Tools for control and implementation

The Board for Promoting Sweden Abroad has overall control of the implementation of the branding strategy, together with the main implementing ministries and government agencies.

As mentioned, two government entities stand out as the most active in the realization of the promotion strategy: the Swedish Institute and Visit Sweden.

The Swedish Institute (SI) is a government agency that has as its main aim to promote interest and trust in Sweden around the world. As such it has a role as one of the main vehicles for Sweden's public diplomacy efforts. It is to some extent the equivalent of national cultural institutes such as Germany's Goethe Institute and the UK's British Council. However, SI does not have representation abroad (apart from one office in Paris) but rather works closely with Swedish embassies and consulates globally.

SI's main tools relate to implementation of the brand strategy focus on communicating Sweden and Swedish skills, experience and values. This is done through a range of digital channels, such as the website sweden.se (available in English, Chinse, Arabic and Russian), different social media channels, the web platform Sharing Sweden, containing easily accessible material and toolkits that Swedish missions abroad and other actors can use to present and talk about the country and Image Bank Sweden, comprising free-of-charge photos that will tell stories about everyday life in Sweden, showcasing themes such as Swedish innovations, sustainability, culture and creativity (the Image Bank Sweden is administered together with Visit Sweden).

SI also continuously monitors Sweden's global image, both by subscribing to some of the main nation brand surveys and by carrying out their own research.

In addition, SI promotes Swedish language learning abroad, manages a number of global talent networks, brings journalists to Sweden and carries out leadership programmes with leaders from all over the world to build long-lasting relations. The leadership programmes are permeated by values that are important to the country, such as human rights and sustainability. Finally, SI is responsible for the international marketing of Sweden as a study destination, in close collaboration with Swedish higher education institutions. This work is guided by the brand strategy – and especially values that relate to being a progressive country are emphasized.

Visit Sweden is the national tourism organization (NTO) of Sweden. From 2020, it is solely owned by the Swedish state (previously 50% by the state and 50% by the Swedish tourism industry).

Visit Sweden do two main things to attract visitors: strive to strengthen the image of the country in general and promote Swedish destinations and experiences with a view to converting interest into bookings. In practical terms, the organization runs marketing campaigns, aiming at making Sweden visible in social media channels, co-operates with tour operators and inspires foreign media to feature Sweden as a travel destination. They also monitor and follow up impact by measuring reach, engagement and the designated target market's claimed preference for Sweden.

A guiding principle for the implementation of the brand strategy is 'show, don't tell,' meaning that promotion efforts should focus on deeds, activities and symbolic actions that help build the desired image, rather than communicating the core values in a more explicit manner.

A case in point is the Curators of Sweden initiative, launched in 2011 and which ran until 2018. Initiated by the Swedish Institute and Visit Sweden, the project handed the official Twitter account @Sweden to a new Swedish person every week, who got to manage it more or less freely, as long as the published views were within the law. The campaign was widely covered in media globally and inspired many similar projects, as well as sparking some controversy when individuals posted sensitive views. The overall goal with the project was to manifest Swedish diversity and progressiveness, and the government agencies rarely corrected any posts, giving them a chance to make a statement and say that any censorship would have been in conflict with precisely the diversity and openness the project wanted to convey in the first place.

A number of other initiatives characterized by the show, don't tell spirit, have subsequently been launched and which also have created publicity worldwide.

Target groups and markets

The official strategy stipulates only one common target group for all promotion efforts: so-called 'connectors'.

Connectors are identified as people possessing large networks in which they are active and spread information and contacts. The idea is that targeting a connector, or someone this person in turn finds interesting, will increase the possibilities of communicating the message to a broader end target group.

It could be a journalist, expert, researcher or opinion-maker. They can also be identified by looking at who has a major impact in social media or the specialist press, or by asking people within a given area who they consider to be a connector. Interestingly, the idea to target connects dates back to the early 2010s, and hence predates the current influencer trend.

In addition, each implementing entity has their own target groups, designated by demography, lifestyle and/or geography. SI, for example, focus their efforts on a target audience of 15- to 35-year-olds, which is a group that is presumed to be more open to move to or study or work in another country.

Visit Sweden, in turn, has chosen a target group labelled the 'Global Traveller' for its marketing campaigns. The target group is described as an experienced traveller who is eager to try new destinations and new experiences. The group tends to take more trips abroad than average, have a higher income and education and is more likely to live in cities.

This target group is further split into three segments with differing motivations for travelling to Sweden: 'Curious Travellers,' 'Outdoor Enthusiasts' and 'Holiday Hedonists'. As for target markets, Visit Sweden have singled out India, United States, China, Germany, the Netherlands, France and Great Britain as prioritized markets. Consequently, these countries are also home to Visit Sweden's overseas offices (apart from India, which is served by the Scandinavian Tourist Board in Delhi).

Visit Sweden has analysed global target markets and come to the conclusion that the Global Traveller target group comprises some 62 million people worldwide, and they are especially found in countries such as Germany and the United States.

Brand architecture

The Swedish brand strategy relies relatively little on city and regional brands. However, a continuous dialogue is held between the national-level agencies and with places, such as innovation hotspots, that help embody what brand Sweden wants to stand for. If a campaign that strives to convey say Swedish innovativeness and design is launched, it could be done in cooperation with the region that is home to a cluster or innovation centre in smart textiles and fashion design.

From a tourism perspective, two regional brands enjoy a special position in the promotion efforts, stemming from the fact they tend to be the two regions that foreigners have heard about before: the capital Stockholm region and the Swedish Lapland region.

In addition, there is also an informal dialogue with major Swedish corporations and brands that explicitly bank on 'Swedishness' and also to some degree develop their own branding strategies from the official promotion strategy, such as Volvo Cars, Absolut Vodka and IKEA.

As for supra-national endorsers, Sweden is a partner in the Nordic countries common branding effort, led by the Nordic Council of Ministers (NCM) and labelled *The Nordics*. The Swedish MFA has a member in the coordinating group that meets regularly to discuss common initiatives, such as joint market research for campaigns. In the last few years, NCM has launched initiatives such as Traces of the North. The initiative rests on the idea of curating Nordic narratives around the world, with the traces reflecting a mix of common values like trust, openness and equality. These could be concepts that are permeated by a unique Nordic twist both physically, such as art and technology, or emotionally, such as expressions of culture, policies and ideas.

In addition, as mentioned earlier, the Scandinavian countries Denmark, Norway and Sweden collaborate under the common umbrella Scandinavian Tourist Board and a common Scandinavian brand in the Indian market.

A commonly used argument and rationale for this type of collaboration is that it is more useful in remote regions, such as Asia and North America, where the general awareness of each individual country in the Nordic regions tends to be lower than in European countries.

On the level of implementation, the Nordic countries can also collaborate in a more ad hoc manner in specific countries, for example by doing a common promotional event or cultural or public diplomacy event. This happens especially in countries such as Germany where the Nordic embassies are co-located in one building in Berlin.

In the same vein, ad hoc event-based collaborations may also take place between EU embassies in a third country, such as organizing an EU film week, even though there is no coordinating taking place on the strategic level.

Lessons learned

A couple of lessons learned stand out from the case. First of all, the consistency and longevity of the strategy, and the stable governance that has been created with the Board for Promoting Sweden Abroad seems to have provided conditions conducive to succeeding in the longer term. The strategy has also survived several governments and been free from any politicization. Promoting the country as an open county that take an active part in dealing with global challenges is a positioning that could have been politically challenged domestically, given how the public discourse around topics such as migration and globalization have shifted the last 4–5 years.

Secondly, the show, don't tell approach has been successful in not only triggering initiatives that have proven successful in their own right, but that also have become viral due to their innovativeness, helping to further validate the core values of innovation, creativeness and progressiveness.

Thirdly, the Swedish effort has been characterized by an evidence-based approach rather than wishful thinking. There is, for example, a consistency and fit between rankings that put Sweden high on measures such as innovation, sustainability and equality and the chosen core values, which probably has given credibility to the strategy.

Sources

Interviews with:
Christian Biller, Brand Manager, Swedish Institute.
Michael Persson Gripkow, Chief Brand and Strategic Marketing Officer, Visit Sweden.
Strategy for the Promotion of Sweden Abroad. https://sharingsweden.se/materials/strategy-promotion-sweden-2-0/, accessed August 5, 2020.

9 Poland

Magdalena Florek and Jarosław Górski

Introduction

According to current rankings of country brands' power (Bloom Consulting Country Brand Ranking 2019/20 – Tourism and Trade editions and Future-Brand Country Index, 2019), Poland belongs to the group of 30% of the strongest country brands in the world and is in the middle of the European ranking.

In this chapter, we go nearly 30 years back to the early 1990s to take a brief look at the branding of Poland. Following the change of system from communism to a free market, the first talks were initiated about the need of building a Polish national brand. The process can be described as a path from chronic shortage to oversupply. Poland has at its disposal numerous planning institutions and documents which make it possible to promote a national brand effectively. Unfortunately, due to insufficient institutional competence (including insufficient coordination of the numerous design activities instigated by public administration, the private sector and public–private organizations), the condition of branding Poland as we know it today is far from excellent. Here we present the major institutions and strategic actions taken for the benefit of building up brand Poland.

Institutions in charge of activities accompanying brand Poland

In the search for a manager of brand Poland and in an attempt to characterize the relations between institutions and programmes aimed at promoting brand Poland, we need to take a close look at the competences in national marketing attributed to various entities on the grounds of the respective common laws.

By virtue of art. 126 of the Constitution of the Republic of Poland, the President represents Poland on the international front – in contacts with

DOI: 10.4324/9781003084051-9

other states and international organizations like NATO and the UN. Promoting Poland in the world also connects with this mission. The acting President of the Republic of Poland has at his disposal initiatives by means of which he tackles the tasks related to promoting Poland abroad:

1) The Entrepreneurship Council – a consultancy and advisory body tasked with establishing a forum for exchanging experiences between scholars (experts in economy and management) and business practitioners. The Entrepreneurship Council includes a Promotion Team and an International Cooperation Team, to name just the two.
2) The Business Prize of the President of the Republic of Poland is a business accolade awarded once a year by the President of the Republic of Poland. The Prize is awarded to the best companies in Poland which contribute to economic growth, promote Poland abroad and serve as models for other businesses.

On the level of the government (Legal act of 4 September 1997 on government administration), the Minister of Foreign Affairs is in charge of promoting Poland abroad by means of (1) creating an international image of the Republic of Poland and (2) involvement in public and cultural diplomacy as well as supporting activities which promote Polish economy, culture, language, tourism, technology and science, pursued by other departments. Notably, nearly all the ministers are responsible for international promotion of Poland in their respective sections of the government administration with the minister in charge of the economy in the lead.

For the ministers to coordinate projects of promoting Poland abroad and creating a robust brand Poland, recently (first quarter 2020) the Prime Minister established two bodies:

1) The Prime Minister's proxy in charge of promotion of the Polish brand as an assisting authority of the Prime Minister.
2) An Inter-ministerial Team in charge of Promotion of the Republic of Poland as an assisting authority of the Council of Ministers, consisting of representatives of nearly all the ministries.

The institutions handling the government's tasks of promoting the Polish economy include the Polish Development Fund (PFR, www.pfr.pl/en/), operating since 2016. It is a Polish joint stock company owned by the State Treasury and Bank Gospodarstwa Krajowego, offering instruments aimed at developing companies, administrative units and private persons, investing in sustainable social development and the country's economic growth. The priorities of the PFR include development of entrepreneurship, exports and expansion of Polish companies abroad, supporting local governments and handling foreign investments. Among the programmes launched by the PFR is *Start in Poland*, centred on supporting by means of internationalization and promotion of innovative Polish companies (including start-ups).

The PFR group consists of, among others, five institutions operating under one brand:

1) The Polish Investment and Trade Agency (PAIH, www.paih.gov.pl) is the key entity in charge of promoting exports and investment. The agency's mission is to increase the impact of foreign direct investment as well as the reach and dynamics of internationalization of Polish companies. The PAIH operates in Poland and with the help of Foreign Trade Offices (ZBH). Interestingly, the agency is a joint stock company (wholly owned by the State Treasury) but, by virtue of a legal act, it is involved in promoting the Polish economy.

2) The goal of the Polish Agency for Enterprise Development (PARP, www.parp.gov.pl) is to implement programmes of developing the economy, supporting innovations and research carried out by small- and medium-sized companies, regional development, boosting exports, development of human resources and use of new technologies in business operations.

3) The Agency for Industrial Development (ARP, www.arp.pl) is a joint stock company supervised by the Prime Minister; it is also wholly owned by the State Treasury. The Agency supports companies in business operations and development thereof as well as in following restructuring processes.

4) Bank Gospodarstwa Krajowego (www.bgk.pl) is tasked with supporting Polish companies in the domestic and the international arenas by means of financial instruments.

5) KUKE (Korporacja Ubezpieczeń Kredytów Eksportowych, www.kuke.com.pl) has insured trade transactions of Polish enterprises for nearly 30 years. KUKE's shareholders include the State Treasury represented by the Prime Minister and Bank Gospodarstwa Krajowego. KUKE offers solutions in the area of supporting exports, elements of 'the state-owned system of exports support'.

Another noteworthy entity is the Polish Centre for Farming Support established in 2017 (KOWR, www.kowr.gov.pl), a state legal entity subordinated to the respective Minister of Rural Development. The KOWR tackles a wide range of tasks previously handled by a few small rural development agencies. According to the establishment act, KOWR's tasks include: (1) involvement in promotion and information activities aimed at promoting agricultural and food products, the methods of production thereof and quality systems of agricultural and food products; and (2) support for the development of trade cooperation in the agricultural and food sectors abroad. The KOWR promotes agricultural and food products in the EU market and beyond and is accompanied by the slogan 'POLAND TASTES GOOD'.

As for institutions undertaking the government's mission of promoting tourism, the Polish Tourism Organization (POT, www.pot.gov.pl/en) is a key entity of the public administration promoting the Polish tourism brand. The POT as Polish Destination Management Organization is a state legal entity established to boost promotion of Poland's tourism in the country and abroad. It operates on the basis of a dedicated legal act and under the supervision of the Minister of Development. In 2011, POT devised a marketing strategy for Polish tourism for 2012–2020. However, the strategy did not solve the issues related to the country brand; instead, it defines the directions of promotion activities. To some extent, the POT strategy was linked and compatible with the governmental development strategies and programmes in public diplomacy, sport, culture, transport and environmental protection. The strategy's mission was defined as 'building and strengthening the image of Poland as attractive and hospitable to tourists, an owner of high quality, competitive tourist products'. The main goals of the strategy include improvement of Poland's competitiveness in domestic and foreign markets, promoting an attractive image of the tourist products, and establishing an efficient tourist information system and transfer of knowledge.

In the area of promoting Polish culture, the most active institutions include:

1   Adam Mickiewicz Institute (IAM, www.iam.pl/en) – a national culture institution with a mission of building and communicating the cultural aspect of brand Poland by means of active participation in international cultural exchange. The Institute has pursued cultural goals in 70 countries. To date, the IAM has presented nearly 5,550 events watched by nearly 52 million spectators on five continents. All the projects managed by the Institute are accompanied by the flagship Culture.pl brand.
2   The National Centre for Culture (NCK, www.nck.pl/en) is a state institute of culture whose statutory responsibility is to develop culture in Poland. The NCK focuses on promoting Polish culture at home although some activities have an international overtone and are complementary to the IAM projects related to the Culture.pl brand.

Among the institutions promoting the Polish national brand is a very large group of entities which are not a part of the system of public administration or operating within public-private partnerships. This group includes primarily the Polish National Foundation (PFN, www.pfn.org.pl) established in 2016 by 16 large state-owned enterprises (from the fuel, power, finance, real estate and armaments industries). The Foundation's mission is to 'promote Polish success in science, the country's rich culture, great history and unique nature'. An analysis of the Foundation's activity suggests that Polish historical policy is the main area of the entity's interest, including promotion of Poland's role in the world. The Foundation's activity has been recently heavily criticized for not having the promotional effect that could be expected with the budget allocated and for politicizing activities.

In Poland there are also a large number of third sector entities such as foundations and associations, oftentimes public-private entities whose founders come from either public administration or business. As part of their statutory activity, they deal with selected aspects of promoting brand Poland. They often operate as think-tanks or different expert organizations, animating public debates, organizing promotion campaigns for specific sectors, events and economic patriotism and holding contests for the best Polish products and services.

Polish local governments are also greatly involved in the promotion, especially on the level of the commune and the province – they devise and implement brand strategies and dedicated development programmes and promotion offers targeted mainly at tourists and local entrepreneurs and, to a lesser extent, at locals and potential investors. While these activities are typically highly professional, they are loosely related to the national branding pursued by public administration on the governmental level.

Comprehensive efforts focused on brand Poland

The first ideas for the country's brand appeared in the early 1990s. The Foundation of the Polish Promotional Emblem, established at that time, started to promote economic patriotism and the Polish brand 'Poland Now,' which was to become a symbol of high-quality Polish products and services (www.terazpolska.pl). Over time, preparations for devising a comprehensive national marketing strategy for Poland started. The project took shape after 2000 when Poland applied for membership of the EU. At that time, the need for defining and promoting Poland's competitive identity became evident.

The first more coherent attempt to create a robust and unique national brand for Poland was initiated by the Polish Chamber of Commerce (www. kog.pl; the biggest independent business organization in Poland, which represents the biggest number of entrepreneurs) and the Institute of Polish Brand (the latter was an independent research and development centre for national and regional branding but it has ceased to exist). In 2003, an international team of consultants led by Wally Olins was commissioned to complete stage one of the project, namely a diagnosis of the Polish national identity and expression of the core idea together with the brand attributes. Stage two consisted of visualization, coordination of messages for the main national brand vectors (tourism, FDI, exports and public diplomacy) as well as designing systems of national brand management (institutional coordination, brand champions/task forces, building support, tracking results, etc.) and was meant to follow shortly. The project was sponsored by the Minister of Economy.

The findings and discussion on the first four ideas characteristic of Polish people and the country led to the core idea expressed in the phrase 'creative tension'. According to Olins, it was the essence of the then Poland – 'Poland draws its personality, power and perpetual motion from a wealth of apparently opposing characteristics. Polish people are idealistic and also pragmatic and resourceful; the Polish character is ambitious and also realistic. Poles are calm and they are also volatile, can be very charming and also tough. Poland is a country driven by these kinds of creative tensions.'

'Creative tension' stimulates a restlessness unsatisfied with the status quo, and a boisterousness that is always stimulating and often astonishing. This creative tension was supposed to explain why Poland produces so many entrepreneurs, artists and sportspeople. It is why Poland constantly changes and evolves, sometimes tumultuously. And this is why Poles have always tried to achieve the seemingly impossible and go their own way – and often succeeded.

The core idea was defined as a starting point, an inspiration for every brand-related activity, for further development of the national brand identity and personality. Unfortunately, the next step did not take place while the subsequent governments were not interested in continuing the project. It was not until 2013 when the marketing sector decided to revive it. The Council for Promoting Poland (including ministers), an advisory body to the Prime Minister which formally coordinated promotion of the country, approved a document, ' "Rules of communication for brand Poland'. It was developed by experts from the Association of Marketing Communication SAR and the Association of Public Relations Companies. In the document, brand Poland was defined as 'a brand providing fresh ideas, experiences and involvement. It sets the tone for the activities, changes its environment, does not leave anyone indifferent'. 'Polska. Spring into new' had become the brand idea. However, a discussion of the document itself centred on the graphic sign representing Poland. Wally Olins was among the designers of the sign – in his opinion, a spring is a good symbol of the nature of Polish people: 'the more we are pressurised, the bigger the pressure, the stronger the reaction to it. This is well reflected in the history of Poland;

Poles often refuse to accept the status quo and enforced rules. They always try to achieve what seems impossible'. The spring symbol was meant to reflect the nature and energy released in Polish people following the transformation of the previous two decades. The idea was that everyone could use the logo free of charge. However, the design has not been implemented on a large scale (the Facebook fanpage dedicated to the 'Polska. Spring into new' brand project has not been active since December 2014 – www.facebook.com/Polska.SpringInto/).

When the ruling party changed, the Intra-governmental Team in Charge of Promoting Poland Abroad operated between 2016 and 2018. The Team consisted of nine task forces. The team adopted two important documents with guidelines for promoting Poland abroad: 'Standardised rules of communicating brand Poland' (2016) and 'Areas of promotion of Poland for 2017–2027' (2017) as well as a document exceeding the promotion aspects; it was an attempt to define a national brand: 'Brand Poland – the concept' (2018) yet still mainly from an external perspective. The document is expected to provide the answers to questions about the nature of brand Poland, its benefits, the most important assumptions and goals of brand Poland, its value, and the relations with other brands. The assumptions of the visual identification system were also outlined together with the rules for introducing and applying the brand, and monitoring and evaluating the results.

According to the assumptions, the concept of brand Poland 'underpins accomplishment of the strategic goals of the Polish State as the sixth biggest and most significant country in the European Union and defending its interests on the international arena'.

Following an analysis of external and internal sources it was concluded that 'Brand Poland is in the initial stage of development, is poorly recognizable and too rarely acknowledged while the problem with perceptions of Poland abroad are not as much negative stereotypes as a general lack of knowledge of Poland'. The desired image among foreign audiences which, according to the authors, stems from genuine premises, is that of 'Poland as a safe, stable and interesting European country with a modern economy and an attractive offer of predictable, high-quality and valuable products and services. As a nation, Poles are entrepreneurial, friendly and open to innovations and foreign contacts, at the same time cherishing their values and rules'.

Hence, as brand essence reflecting its spirit, the authors suggested 'Safety and opportunities'. In relation to this definition, the following brand values have been identified (notably, these are direct references to the features of brand personality) (see Figure 9.1 for summary):

a) Innovative – provides ideas and solutions; as a result, the world is a better place.

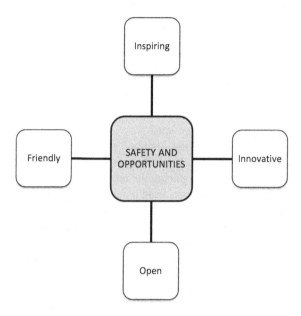

Figure 9.1 The suggested concept of brand Poland – brand essence and brand values
Source: 'Brand Poland – the Concept' (2018, p. 43).

This pertains to the mode of thinking, operating, meeting challenges and coming up with non-standard solutions, in the economy as well as in the social, political, civilization and humane aspects. It combines Poland's heritage and the contribution of illustrious Poles (inventors, thinkers, leaders, philosophers, etc.) to the development of world civilization. It promotes wide-ranging Polish achievements. This value is defined by the following features: entrepreneurial, ingenious, courageous, active, resourceful.

b) Inspiring – releases human energy, stimulates to act and share achievements.

   It assumes an active attitude towards any challenges and motivates to act. It inspires creativity and supports out-of-the-box approaches to any challenges coupled with creative and effective solutions. It shows how to meet the challenges of the future in a creative way. This value is defined by the following features: creative, engaging, imaginative, exciting, motivating.

c) Open – easily accessible to anyone and open to human interests and needs.

It emphasizes the willingness to learn and master one's skills. Open also means wise, intelligent, capable of easy adaptation to changing conditions and rising to new challenges in an open way. However, it does not indicate uncritical acceptance of anything that appears new. It draws on history but goes out to the world with its message. It is frank and straightforward in expressing opinions. This value is defined by the following features: authentic, spontaneous, kind, helpful, joyful.

d)   Friendly – tells a story about people, their relations, shared experience of important and happy moments.

It gives a sense of safety, stability and predictability. It is based on the heritage and the rich tradition as well as the universal values which make it possible to pursue the most significant human needs in a responsible way. Its charm, friendliness and willingness to help are attributed to the traditional Polish hospitality and family-orientation. It is reliable and trustworthy. This value is defined by the following features: family-oriented, safe, hospitable, loyal, honest.

At the latest stage of development of brand Poland, the authors of the document 'Rules of communication of brand Poland' recommend that communication of brand Poland is based on the following concepts: (a) innovations and development, (b) heritage and contribution to the world's civilization, (c) cultural openness, and (d) people. The story revolving around brand Poland – based on the brand values and promise – should be modern yet refer to the cultural heritage and values.

Brand Poland is meant to be always the main brand, superior to the sector-related brands (tourism, science, exports, investments, culture) which in this respect are sub-brands. Brand Poland is also superior to the brands of business or tourist organizations; cultural or educational institutions; special events (exhibitions, concerts, anniversaries); cities and regions; commercial brands, and so on. In this model, many partner organizations instigate activities under a single 'umbrella'.

According to the document, there is a need for well-thought and coherent visual identification of brand Poland. It should replace the numerous, oftentimes coexisting visualizations which lessen an effective impact on the audience. Except for the concepts which need to be used for formal reasons, for example, projects sponsored with EU funds, the remaining concepts should be replaced by new and standardized visualization.

As for organizing the process of building brand Poland, establishment of a 'Brand Poland Office' should be considered. This office must not operate as a foundation or a public-private partnership because it would not have the desired power of carrying out decisions and standards. It should be established at the very beginning of work on the brand, that is, making the strategic decision rather than at a later stage. A formalized and centrally agreed solution was recommended because – while regular consultations with various social or business groups are imperative – brand Poland itself must be managed by an authority capable of enforcing the required decisions, supervising implementation thereof, signing the required contracts, initiating and comprehensibly coordinating activities and expecting implementation thereof.

An optimum solution, recommended in the document, is for the Brand Poland Office to attract partners represented by research institutions, universities and/or think-tanks and trade organizations which, for example as honorary brand patrons, would help to define objective criteria and indicators as part of non-profit activities and to carry out research and evaluate items dedicated to brand Poland (it is recommended to establish approximately 30 most important measures including the major areas of operation of brand Poland, among them the country's perceived technological, economic and social advancement; the importance of the label 'Polish product'; attractiveness of investing, studying, visiting and living in the country; perception of Poles; evaluation of the role and impact of Polish culture abroad).

The Intra-governmental Team in Charge of Promoting Poland Abroad has finished its work with the document 'Directions of Promotion of Poland in 2017–2027'. As a direction document, it contains general guidelines and rules and it defines the major areas of promoting Poland abroad. The document describes the areas, goals, tactics and examples of promotion activities underpinning accomplishment of long- and medium-term goals set by Poland's key strategic documents.

Final reflections

Since the beginning of the system transformation in the late 1980s and the early 1990s, there has been awareness of the need to promote Poland abroad in a systematic, well-organized way. The first attempts at creating a strategic framework for brand Poland were strictly related to the country's accession to the EU; it was stimulated by the private sector represented by the Polish Chamber of Commerce. In the past two decades, several strategic documents were drawn up in Poland with the aim of identifying and providing more details and interpreting the identity of brand Poland and its major instruments (especially the system of visual identification and the communication guidelines).

However, the content-related solutions defining brand Poland were not accompanied by satisfactory work on institutionalizing and operationalizing these processes. As discussed previously, the numerous branding projects developed by the state administration, local governments and stimulated by private as well as public-private entities – including projects for promoting the Polish economy, tourism and culture in the world, sponsored by the EU – within 2 decades caused a transition from a shortage to an excess of concepts and solutions. This is particularly visible in the numerous co-existing systems of the country's visual identification. Six logos are/ were used to promote Poland: (1) The logo used by the Ministry of Foreign Affairs to promote Poland abroad after 2002, (developed for 1 Polish Zloty by Corporate Profile DD); (2) Logo of Poland designed by Saffron Brand Consultants and commissioned by the Association of Marketing Communication SAR, adopted as an official logo of Poland in 2014 by the Council for Promoting Poland; (3) Polish Economy logo created as part of the government's project of promoting the Polish economy abroad (2018, p. 4) Logo used by the Polish Investment and Trade Agency (formerly the Polish Information and Investment Agency) to promote investments in Poland; (5) The Poland logo referred to by the Polish Tourist Organization as a 'tourist quality mark' and made available to other entities exclusively to promote Polish tourism in foreign markets and in the domestic market as specified in an ordinance of the Ministry of Economy; and (6) Logo indicating products and services from Poland, made available to the winners of the 'Teraz Polska' (Poland Now competition).

The identity of brand Poland evolved from the original one ranging from eastern traditions to western aspirations to brand identity with emphasis placed on the affinity with the European cultural heritage as well as accomplishments in the economy and culture. The key values of brand Poland are now inspirational nature, openness, friendliness and innovations. Promotion of the country's brand has become a political issue looked after by the government. However, the effectiveness of the coordination efforts is rather poor; it is additionally impacted by the highly political decision-making process and public diplomacy strongly affecting the image of brand Poland. Despite the fact that no transparent instruments of coordinated promotion of brand Poland have been introduced, the key initiatives launched to promote tourism, culture, exports and investment connect well with the general assumptions about the competitive identity of brand Poland.

Bibliography

'Brand Poland – the Concept'. (2018) *Inter-Ministerial Team in Charge of Promotion of the Republic of Poland Abroad*, Warsaw.

'Directions of Promotion of Poland in 2017–2027'. (2017) *Inter-Ministerial Team in Charge of Promotion of the Republic of Poland Abroad*. Minister of Foreign Affairs, Warsaw.

Legal Act of 4 September 1997 on the Departments of Government Administration (Official Journal 2020, Items 1220, 1087).

'Rules of Communication for Brand Poland'. (2013) Minister of Foreign Affairs, Warsaw.

'Standardised Rules of Communicating Brand Poland'. (2016) *Inter-Ministerial Team in Charge of Promotion of the Republic of Poland Abroad*. Minister of Foreign Affairs, Warsaw.

10 The Netherlands

Robert Govers and Simon Anholt

In 2004 the Dutch Society and Business Foundation (Stichting Maatschappij en Onderneming) published a booklet entitled *Branding NL*. It includes several theoretical contributions; from the reputable Clingendael – Netherlands Institute of International Relations (notably Peter van Ham and Jan Melissen), as well as the late branding pundit Wally Olins. Most importantly though, the last chapter incorporates the 'brand strategy advice' provided by the Holland Image working group that convened in 2003. The working group and subsequent *Branding NL* symposium that took place on 17 November 2004 included representatives of the – then – Economic Diplomacy Service (EVD, now RVO); Ministry of Foreign Affairs; Ministry of Agriculture; Ministry of Infrastructure and Water Management; Government Information Service; Clingendael Institute; Netherlands Board of Tourism & Conventions (NBTC); Netherlands Foreign Investment Agency (NFIA); Netherlands Universities Foundation for International Cooperation (NUFFIC, which is now the Dutch organization for internationalization in education); Centre for International Cultural Activities (SICA, now Dutch-Culture); Radio Netherlands World Service; Amsterdam Partners, Royal Association MKB-Nederland (for SMEs); and the Confederation of Netherlands Industry and Employers (VNO-NCW).

It was quite an early attempt for a nation state government administration and its stakeholders – with such a wide representation – to start thinking seriously about an overarching, inter-ministerial and nation-wide country brand initiative and calling it such. This was early, because the first musings about 'the nation as brand' were only published around the turn of the century, some most notably by one of the co-authors of this contribution. Earlier, in the late eighties and nineties, academics and practitioners discussed 'place branding' in the context of investment promotion and tourism ('destination branding'). This was also the case in the Netherlands where, in 1987, the Bureau for Tourism had already decided to use a tulip as its logo and the 'brand name' Holland. The tulip logo that was used until recently

DOI: 10.4324/9781003084051-10

was then commissioned by the Bureau for Tourism and designed by famous Dutch designer Ton Giesbergen in 1996. However, the idea of managing the overall image of the country internationally was quite novel at the time.

In *Branding NL* (2004) the working group argued that there was an urgent need – in 2003 – for intervention. Even though a 2001 study commissioned by the Ministry for Foreign Affairs showed that the image of the country abroad was quite positive, major news events undermined Dutch confidence. In 2002 the Dutch government resigned over the findings of the Dutch Institute for War Documentation into the Srebrenica Massacre. The maverick politician Pim Fortuyn was assassinated in broad daylight by animal rights activist Volkert van der Graaf. Fortuyn's new populist party still won the general election, forming a new government that fell a second time in the same year as a result of infighting among the newcomers. These events seemed to fuel a general sentiment that something needed to be done to take control of the image of the Netherlands abroad.

The working group, which, incidentally, was again chaired and initiated by the Bureau for Tourism, formulated the following recommendations in 2004:

1 Deploy a cohesive communication strategy;
2 Develop a brand strategy using the brand logo (the orange tulip) and the name *Holland*. It was argued that even though the official name of the country is *the Kingdom of the Netherlands* (which should be upheld), market research showed that *Holland* has higher name awareness and is easier to remember and pronounce for most foreigners and therefore should be formally recognized as a brand name;
3 Select relevant target audiences;
4 Enhance collaboration and – within that context – strengthen the consultative role of the Holland Image working group;
5 Have government strive towards an integrated and unified external communications policy;
6 Involve the Ministry of Education, Culture and Sciences and other agencies in the external communication efforts;
7 Bundle image campaigns together;
8 Assign a central role to the internet in the external communication efforts;
9 Strengthen traditional information carriers;
10 Organize effective information management;
11 Organize joint relationship management;
12 Organize joint event management;
13. Prepare risk management scenarios in case of negative publicity incidents.

The defining purpose of the Netherlands

The Netherlands is a country that competes and collaborates at the same time; through enlightened self-interest it builds mutually beneficial partnerships to come up with pragmatic multidisciplinary solutions that build a better future for all.

This defining purpose needs to be understood in the following context:

- This is not just about economic prosperity. As it has done in the past, the Netherlands also aims to contribute to global rule of law, peace and security, culture, technological advancement, social equality and environmental sustainability;
- This is done through collaboration and co-operation; collaboration internationally as well as between public, private and civil society actors.

The ambition of the Netherlands

Co-creating pioneering solutions to global challenges
In our international engagement, what we in the Netherlands *value*, is[1]*:*

- To seek win–win–win[2] multidisciplinary collaboration (inclusiveness)
- To find out-of-the-box, yet pragmatic solutions (inventiveness)
- While cherishing freedom, transparency and boldness (openness)

It is clear that in these early days 'nation branding,' promotion, public relations, public diplomacy, visual identity and sectoral marketing were frequently conflated, but in any case, very little happened after the publication of these recommendations. There was hardly any follow-up and the Holland Image working group was disbanded in 2004. Visual identity and promotional initiatives were implemented in tourism, export and investment promotion. The Bureau for Tourism owned and licenced the orange Holland tulip logo (with an official adoption of the logo for promotional purposes by the central government in 2009). In 2005–2006 the then State Secretary for Economic Affairs Van Gennip initiated an economic image management policy. Co-author of this chapter, Simon Anholt, consulted on this. Yet, an overarching, nation-wide brand strategy never materialized until 2018, when the authors of this contribution were asked to assist in a new project, managed by the Ministry of Foreign Affairs. This was the result of years of lobbying by the Holland Branding working group that was – yet again – convened by the Bureau for Tourism (initially in 2014).

In 2018, a steering group (mostly government) and an advisory group were convened, consisting of approximately the same set of stakeholders represented earlier in the Holland Image working group, with the addition of representatives of various leading economic sectors, the Dutch Trade Board, Eindhoven 365, Rotterdam The Hague Region Marketing, National Olympic Committee and the Association of Dutch Museums and Attraction Parks. Again, the initiative was successful in bringing together a very broad representation of relevant societal actors.

After many consultative meetings the following strategy was formulated.

In terms of targeting, the project argued that there is no such need, initially. 'Nation branding' is about orchestrating, as much as possible, a consistent positioning in all the various ways in which the Netherlands engages with the outside world (in Europe and beyond). The aim was to have the positioning strategy provide focus to as many initiatives as possible. Of course, specific projects, products and policies have their own internal objectives, aims and target audiences, and at that level segmentation should be considered, but in a way that still reflects the overarching strategy. How this is done is a matter of implementation, but should not determine the overall strategy, which should resonate in almost everything and with almost everyone in the country.

Implementation of the aforementioned strategy required additional effort. It needed to build or reinforce more future-oriented supporting evidence; substance and what one of the co-authors of this chapter, Simon Anholt, has termed 'Symbolic Actions'. Additional effort was to be put into the implementation of the strategy in terms of policies in relation to the organizational framework, governance, ownership and collaboration with externally facing Dutch agencies and at scalar levels (geographically). Furthermore, there was a need for a framework for impact measurement and accountability. So far it is unclear what the future implementation plan might be or how progress is monitored and controlled.

What did happen in 2019 is that, as an add-on to the above brand strategy, the government agencies involved in the project decided that a new visual identity was needed and a new orange logo, with the tulip integrated in the letters NL, was introduced. In addition, it was stated that all government agencies should use the official name of the Kingdom of the Netherlands or The Netherlands for short, in all their communication. Finally, in November 2019, the Minister for Foreign Trade and Development Cooperation launched all of this – the strategy and logo – at a press conference in The Hague. As predicted, this did not produce the desired enthusiasm.

The core idea that the brand strategy was about 'on-brand' collaborative action – projects, investments, policies, events – remained largely unnoticed in the public debate that emerged following the press conference. Even though the nation brand initiative hosts a commendable NL brand platform (www.nlplatfrom.nl coordinated by the Dutch Ministry of Foreign Affairs and delivered by the Netherlands Enterprise Agency), listing many 'on-brand' initiatives that support the strategy, most of the Dutch (social) media talked about the new logo. The brand strategy was pushed far into the background.

Worse still, all that the international media would talk about was the naming convention. The headlines were telling. 'Why Dutch Officials Want You to Forget the Country of Holland' (the *New York Times*).[3] 'We Are The Netherlands: Dutch Government Ditches Holland Brand' (Forbes).[4] 'Dutch government ditches Holland to rebrand as the Netherlands' (The Guardian).[5] 'Netherlands drops 'Holland' in rebranding move' (BBC).[6] 'The Netherlands sheds its "Holland" nickname in the new year' (Lonely Planet).[7] 'The Netherlands reveals new identity and drops "Holland" for good' (Design Week).[8] Most reports light-heartedly poked a little fun at the idea that a government should tell people in other countries how to address them, despite language, historical and cultural differences. The undertone was somewhat derogatory, instead of praising a strategy that aims for laudable international collaboration, it seemed to suggest that the Dutch were navel-gazing.

It turned out that a participant in one of the working groups had leaked an incomplete account of the new brand strategy, months before the official press conference.[9] This was picked up by the international media and spread like wildfire, all platforms referencing each other without much investigative journalism. At the same time, the minister and her spokespersons were unable to bring any nuance to the story.

It is one of those clear examples that reveal the complexity and sensitivity of 'nation branding': the focus on logo and naming was unnecessary, unproductive and irrelevant. The idea that The Netherlands should be used as the official name alongside the new visual identity was 'just' an internal government decision, applicable only to official government agencies. It was never intended to become legislation for the whole country to adhere to. In fact, the Bureau for Tourism found itself compelled to release a public statement[10] explaining that it would continue to use the name Holland abroad, whenever this was seen to be most effective.

The 2018 project report clearly stated that 'the steering committee decided that in relation to the naming convention 'The Netherlands' is preferred. However, the name Holland is perfectly acceptable if the domains in which specific organizations are active, local circumstances, languages or audiences require a different approach. Nevertheless, the national government should use the official name of The Netherlands. The rationale is that there is one official name used by the United Nations, Google, in league tables (FIFA, Olympics) and the international English-language protocol, which is "The Netherlands".' There was no question of the kind of diktat suggested by the international media, and in point of fact, official government agencies, embassies, ministries or representations in official international organizations have always used the official name of the Kingdom of the Netherlands, unless otherwise dictated by the local language (e.g. in Mandarin Chinese the official name *is* 'Holland').

In other words: much ado about nothing. Yet, in the meantime, as happens so often, the brand strategy, and what 'nation branding' should really be about, remains misunderstood. Strangely, the topic seems to arouse little or no curiosity in the media: it merely serves as an excuse to hint at the arrogance or foolishness of government officials the world over, and to enhance a few lazy stereotypes. It is very conceivable that many in the Netherlands – policy makers, politicians, elites, administrators, economic actors and the general public – will now say 'we have a brand, job done' whilst the systems, structures and resources that are needed for 'proper nation branding' – the implementation, brand management, brand architecture, monitoring – continue to be inadequate. The idea of a strategic 'Holland brand' initiative has probably been contaminated yet again and might take another 15 years for it to resurface on the government's agenda.

Notes

1 It is important to note here that these 'values' are 'added values', not 'cultural values'; not a description of who the Dutch are, but what they have to offer to the world. In fact, none of the above (purpose, ambition, values) should be seen as 'branding' in the limited sense of guidelines for all marketing communication. It is a guide to synergistic action, which needs to be implemented through real substance and Symbolic Actions; and if so desired, reflected in the marketing programmes of externally facing agencies and other relevant stakeholders where appropriate.
2 For the benefit of all partners, society and the planet.
3 www.nytimes.com/2020/01/13/world/europe/holland-netherlands-new-name.html
4 www.forbes.com/sites/davidnikel/2019/10/05/its-netherlands-not-holland-dutch-government-decides/
5 www.theguardian.com/world/2019/oct/04/holland-the-netherlands-dutch-government-rebrand
6 www.bbc.com/news/blogs-news-from-elsewhere-49921029

7 www.lonelyplanet.com/articles/holland-netherlands-rebrand-2020
8 www.designweek.co.uk/issues/11-17-november-2019/netherlands-logo/
9 www.adformatie.nl/merkstrategie/nederland-vervangt-merk-holland-door-
   netherlands#comments
10 www.nbtc.nl/nl/home/organisatie/reactie-nbtc-t.a.v.-lancering-nieuwe-neder
   land-branding.htm

11 Ireland

Mark Henry[1]

Introduction

Ireland has a strong nation brand for a small place. The Republic of Ireland has a population of just 5 million people and shares the island with Northern Ireland, part of the United Kingdom. Yet the Anholt-GfK Nation Brands Index consistently places Ireland amongst the 'teens' of most positively considered nation brands for the past couple of decades.[2]

FutureBrand's Country Brand Index 2014–15 ranked Ireland 21st out of 75 countries, ahead of much more populous states such as Spain, Greece, Argentina, Thailand and Turkey.[3] Brand Finance rates Ireland as the 26th most valuable nation brand out of the top 100, above other wealthy nations such as Qatar, Luxembourg, Norway, Denmark and New Zealand.[4]

The Good Country Index ranks Ireland as the 3rd best country in the world in terms of its contribution to the common good of humanity.[5] When the index first launched in 2014, Ireland was ranked first out of 125 countries.

What has Ireland done to deserve such high billing?

It helps that Ireland has a large diaspora. One in ten Americans identify themselves as having Irish ancestry – that is 32 million people.[6] One in ten Britons have at least one grandparent born in Ireland.[7] Add 4.6 million Canadians and 2 million Australians and the sum dwarfs the number of those living on the island of Ireland today.[8] This global audience generally views Ireland fondly and is proud of its Irish heritage. They are likely to speak well of the country in any survey asking for their views of various nations.

Ireland is also Europe's shining star. It has transformed from the poorest nation in the European Economic Community when it joined in 1973, to being one its very richest in the European Union today.[9] It experienced an astonishing period of economic growth in the late 1990s and early 2000s that averaged over 6% per annum and helped to nearly double the numbers in employment. The country was hit hard by the Great Recession, but by the

DOI: 10.4324/9781003084051-11

end of the 2010s the economy was matching or outperforming its previous record highs on most metrics.

Furthermore, Ireland has won the Eurovision song contest more than any other nation; given birth to Riverdance, the world's most successful dance production; and is home to Ryanair, which has transformed travel and tourism for the whole continent. As a former colony – never a coloniser – the country has done little to damage its relationship with other nations and populaces besides. What's not to like?

Ireland's historical brand architecture

It has been argued that Ireland's brand image emerged in its present form at the end of the 19th century.[10] Although there were no marketing gurus around to talk about 'brand' at the time, the country's image conceivably emerged as a result of a deliberate and conscious effort on the part of a group of intellectuals, the most active and influential being the poet and Nobel Laureate W.B. Yeats.

Roy Foster's biography of Yeats makes it clear that he wanted Ireland to 'lead the way in a war on materialism, decadence and triviality, as well as affirming her own individuality – Ireland's spiritual idealism must be forged into a new world outlook for the dawning century'.[11] The country's 'brand image' was to be one of ancient spirituality, mysticism, Gaelic, romance, community, sociability, and a closeness to nature rather than industry. In part, this was designed as a deliberate counterweight to the perceived materialistic and modernistic society of Great Britain – Ireland's dominant neighbour and governor at the time.

Any brand image cannot hold for long if it is not credible. There was, of course, an element of truth in it all. However, the proposition arrived in time to intertwine with the Gaelic revival movement and the demands for independence that led to the creation of Ireland as a free state in 1922. Subsequent political leaders nourished the idea of a distinctive and noble Irish identity that stemmed from a time before Britain had started ruling the country.

The image resonated well amongst the global diaspora. Their ancestors had, in the main, left Ireland in the second half of the 19th century or the early part of the 20th century and departed a rural, non-industrialized country where community bonds ran deep. The diaspora in turn became brand ambassadors, spreading the word of this old Ireland through the communities in which they now resided.

When the country established its national tourism organization in 1952, it was christened 'Bord Fáilte' – the 'Welcome Board' in Gaelic – to reinforce and further propagate the brand image overseas. It made good use of the image in its communications for several decades, even reprinting 1920s romanticized paintings of rural landscapes in its promotional work in the 1960s.

It is unsurprising, therefore, that this well-ingrained brand image of Ireland was slow to evolve over the years. Of the six major criteria assessed by the Nations Brand Index, it is 'tourism' and 'people' that citizens of other nations rate Ireland strongest for today.[12] Ireland's highest ranked individual brand attributes are 'natural beauty' and 'welcoming people' – just as they would have been in the Nations Brand Index of 1922, had it been around.

Ireland's current brand architecture

The national brand of Ireland is not one that is managed centrally. There is no single brand narrative for the country as a whole. There is no pan-sectoral national promotional agency or advertising campaign.

It is unmanaged at a national level, and yet it has proved extraordinarily successful in delivering social and economic benefit where it matters. The success has been through the adoption of sectoral branding approaches that have proved fit for purpose in driving standout growth in tourism, in food and drink production, and in foreign direct investment in particular. These three leading export-orientated sectors, combined, are the source of most of Ireland's employment.[13]

Ireland is amongst the world's leading tourism destinations when judged by the number of international visitors per resident.[14] The country exports 90% of the food it produces, helping it to become, for example, the largest net exporter of beef in the northern hemisphere and the source of over 10% of the world's infant formula.[15] And Ireland is one of the most successful countries in attracting foreign direct investment (FDI) over a sustained period, with the resultant jobs being more valuable than those generated in any other country on the planet.[16]

It can be argued that each of these sectors has benefited from the country's historic brand image. Tourism and food production leverage rural imagery to great effect, and our people are central to the country's competitive advantage in attracting FDI. However, the national promotional agency for each sector adopted a sophisticated approach, sustained over many years, to influencing their discrete target audiences to choose Ireland or Irish produce over those of other locations.

Tourism Brand Ireland

'Tourism Brand Ireland' came into existence in the mid-1990s with the support of European Union funding. It was a cross-border initiative, promoting overseas tourism to both the Republic of Ireland and Northern Ireland under the one banner of the island of Ireland. This jurisdictional cooperation was formalized in the establishment of Tourism Ireland as a cross-border body to take on responsibility for the brand and for overseas promotion of both countries from 2002.

Over the course of nearly three decades, Tourism Brand Ireland has evolved subtly as consumer preferences and the holiday experiences on the island have changed. The initial brand model focused on the welcome of the people, the beautiful landscape of the place and the slower pace of life on the island. However, as Ireland's 'Celtic Tiger' economic boom took hold in the late 1990s and 2000s so the claim to a slower pace of life became less credible and this was replaced by culture.[17]

Periodic reviews, involving global consumer research and stakeholder consultations, have resulted in subsequent evolutions of the brand. The current proposition rests on two pillars: the 'characters' of the people and the 'character' of the place, and there has been a shift from a product-centric architecture to one that is consumer-centric with the brand benefit of an Ireland holiday identified as 'joyful immersion'.[18]

Tourism Ireland invests more than any other arm of the Irish state in promoting the country's image. With annual marketing budgets ranging from €40 million to €60 million, it is the only agency that engages in direct consumer communications of any significant weight.[19] This involves above-the-line marketing activity, such as TV and cinema advertising, in Great Britain, France, Germany and the United States. Online promotion also takes place in these markets and a dozen others, supported by comprehensive publicity programmes and cooperative promotion with trade.

The agency aims to positively influence consumer perceptions of the island of Ireland as a holiday destination and sets targets for short-term and longer-term intentions to holiday here amongst consumers in its key markets. Progress is assessed annually through multi-market brand tracking surveys.

The agency's success has been widely recognized internationally. The World Economic Forum, for instance, has ranked Ireland as the third best country in the world in the 'effectiveness of marketing and branding to attract tourists' in its most recent review of global tourism competitiveness.[20]

Food Brand Ireland

'Food Brand Ireland' was created by Bord Bia, the state's food and drink export promotion agency, in 2010.[21] The initial brand concept rested, as its sister tourism brand did, on the place and the culture of Ireland. These came together to deliver remarkable produce that was natural, diverse, local and authentic.[22]

The food brand landscape was enhanced by the development of the world's first national sustainability programme for agriculture and food by Bord Bia, labelled 'Origin Green' and launched in 2012. The programme sought to support the country's claim to more sustainable means of production as a source of competitive advantage. Approximately 95% of dairy farmers and 85% of beef farmers have committed to delivering independently benchmarked improvements in environmental impacts, animal welfare, energy usage and biodiversity. Together with food processor participation, 90% of Ireland's food exports are now assessed on their sustainability performance.[23]

After an early effort to build brand equity in Origin Green as a unifying differentiator for the sector, Bord Bia now utilize both Origin Green and a quality mark as proof points that engender trust in the overall Food Brand Ireland proposition. The current proposition was evolved in 2017 following research amongst stakeholders at home, and consumers and trade in 13 global markets. The essence of the proposition is 'our nature nurtured,' supported by a range of proof points about both the place the product originates from and the product itself. These include the landscape, the ocean, the clean air and the more sustainable means of food production, leading to taste and nutritional benefits.

Bord Bia invests directly in building consumer brand awareness and propensity to purchase through above-the-line communications such as TV in Germany, Italy and the Netherlands, supported by an increasing amount of digital activity. However, the majority of its brand marketing is through integrated B2B campaigns across digital platforms, print media and physical touchpoints such as face-to-face customized events, missions and trade fairs.

Unlike in the tourism sector, Irish food and drink companies engage in significant consumer and trade promotion directly in international markets. Food Brand Ireland is available for them to leverage in their own communications and this is supported by Bord Bia through brand guidelines and a toolkit of assets to ensure communications alignment.

Periodic research with consumers and trade in key markets assesses the desirability of these proof points, the credibility of Irish produce in claiming these proofs, and the value that Irish produce is seen to offer. These measures are assessed at an overall level and are supported by sectoral specific assessments, for example for beef, dairy produce or seafood.

Foreign direct investment

The attraction of foreign investment to drive the country's industrialization and exports has been government policy since the 1950s. Ireland's key selling proposition in the early decades was a competitively low corporate tax rate of 10%. In the 1970s and 1980s this proposition was broadened to highlight the availability of a young, highly educated, English-speaking workforce as employees to firms moving into the European market. The promotional campaigns then undertaken by the Industrial Development Authority – the national investment promotion and development agency – were titled 'We are the Young Europeans'.[24]

As firms experienced continued success in locating to Ireland, in particular with the introduction of the Single European Market in 1992, so the range of proof points available to promote Ireland expanded. IDA Ireland (as the Industrial Development Authority is now known) operates exclusively in a B2B environment. Its brand architecture is, therefore, focused more on rational proof points than on emotive communications.

Its current architecture was developed following extensive staff and client consultations, with the involvement of communications agencies, and is designed to support its 5-year strategy out to 2024. Its eight pillars include Ireland's stable economic and political environment, the ease of doing business here, the access to talent and a highly educated workforce, the country's track record as a successful location for FDI, and the fact that it is an EU member. The competitive corporate tax rate is now a proof point for the ease of doing business rather than a standalone pillar.

Internal communications guidelines ensure consistency in the brand application, while also allowing flexibility for aspects to be dialled up or down depending on the client or sector. The brand is expressed through integrated campaigns that include face-to-face communications, events, publicity and social media, with digital advertising playing an increasing role in recent years. As IDA Ireland's organizational targets relate to the number of projects landed and jobs created, brand perceptions and communications metrics are secondary.

Other expressions of Brand Ireland

There are, of course, other arms of the Irish state that promote aspects of the country in support of their remits. Culture Ireland supports performances of Irish art and culture internationally. Enterprise Ireland helps indigenous companies grow their export business. Science Foundation Ireland encourages global STEM talent to work with Irish researchers, helps build recognition of Irish research internationally and fosters global collaboration.

The most omnipresent arm of the Irish state is, nevertheless, its diplomatic network. Ireland has diplomatic relations with 161 other countries and a network of 90 embassies and consulates and missions.[25] Diplomats play a coordinating role in the promotion of the country in their geography, typically convening 'Team Ireland' meetings of the state agencies active in their territory to identify synergies and to coordinate activities around major events such as the Saint Patrick's Day national holiday.

Cross-agency cooperation is common on projects where branding opportunities exist for each separate agency or where there is a recognition that, by working together, a greater impact can be delivered for the country as a whole. Examples include the 'Global Greening' initiative whereby international landmarks are illuminated in green – Ireland's national colour – in recognition of Saint Patrick's Day.[26] Tourism Ireland and the Department of Foreign Affairs, in particular, cooperate to recruit new locations every year and to highlight the occasion to their audiences.

Government trade missions will typically seek to identify beneficial opportunities that a Minister's presence in the country can offer to a range of state agencies. The country's presence at world fairs and expos are multi-agency affairs, as evidenced by Bord Bia taking the lead in developing the content for the Expo 2015 pavilion in Milan with input from Tourism Ireland. Ad hoc project teams will also come together to maximize the opportunities of occasional events as they arise. For example, a multi-agency video promoting Ireland in Japanese was created for the Rugby World Cup 2019 when the Irish team met the hosts, Japan.

Relationships to sub- and supra-brands

Ireland is a small country with only the capital city, Dublin, having in excess of 1 million residents. Dublin City and some other metropolitan areas and regions have invested in the development of their own distinct brands. Generally speaking, these are orientated towards domestic audiences with little investment in international promotion. These locations typically feature in the tourism or investment promotion of the national agency overseas without utilization of their brand logo or slogans. However, regional proof points or messaging will be represented in communications where they add value and offer points of differentiation. In the tourism space, for example, the country has been carved into four 'experience brands' which highlight discrete reasons to visit each region.[27]

Reference to European Union membership varies by sector, depending on its relevance. EU membership is one of the core pillars of IDA Ireland's brand architecture as access to the European market remains amongst the primary reasons firms will establish operations here. In food and tourism promotion, on the other hand, its primary value is in locating the country geographically in distant markets where awareness of the country is starting from a low base. Identifying Ireland specifically as an island off the edge of Europe has been utilized in both food and tourism communications to assist with branding the country as an unspoilt, coastal and predominantly rural place.

The future for Brand Ireland

Historical Brand Ireland has served the country well. It has provided a strong basis for tourism and food promotion – which leverage the imagery of rural landscapes – and for attracting inward investment – which leverages the image of an engaging people. However, the ability of the historical positioning to survive unaltered for another century has been challenged.[28]

Ireland's diaspora is primarily located in the Anglo-centric world. This proved enormously advantageous as the United States became the preeminent economic power of the 20th century and provided Ireland with her greatest single source of FDI and of tourism revenue. The economic growth of Asia in the 21st century will dilute this advantage and will require the country to develop much greater levels of brand recognition in places in which it currently has little currency.

The Anholt-GfK Nation Brands Index furthermore shows that even in these Anglo-centric nations, Ireland's brand strength is strongest amongst older cohorts and weakest amongst the youngest. There is a job to be done to shore up positive perceptions in these traditional markets to ensure they remain equally strong advocates into the future, and therefore as strong a source of investment and export earnings.

The historical image of Ireland is also increasingly out of touch with today's reality. Although it remains more rural than many other European nations, nevertheless it is a predominantly urban country nowadays with a GDP per capita that exceeds nearly every European peer.[29] The historical brand image is, therefore, increasingly incongruous and too narrow to reflect the diversity of modern Ireland.

Would Brand Ireland, therefore, benefit from a more coordinated national narrative and the creation of a brand architecture to sit above the sectoral work of individual agencies?

The government of Ireland believes so. In 2018 the Taoiseach (Prime Minister) announced an initiative to double Ireland's global footprint in the period to 2025. As encapsulated in the policy document 'Global Ireland – Ireland's Global Footprint to 2025,' there is now a government commitment to 'implement a global communications strategy that is co-ordinated across all relevant stakeholders in order to present a unified image of Ireland as a good place in which to live, work, do business, invest and visit'.[30]

In countries where Ireland is effectively unknown, a national brand narrative may succeed more effectively than a sectoral one, paving the way for tourism and investment promotion to follow. It also has to be recognized that, as effective as the Irish state agencies have been in developing their own sectors, it is in their interest to only focus on the aspects of the nation brand that are relevant to their domains. It is not in any one of their remits to paint a complete picture of the nation, aside from the Department of Foreign Affairs which has other priorities besides.

To be successful, such an initiative will require sufficiently impactful investment combined with brand guidelines that add value to, rather than confuse or diminish, the successful sectoral model that has worked so well in markets where the Ireland brand is already well established.

Furthermore, as Simon Anholt observes: 'national images are not created through communications, and cannot be altered by communications'.[31] Rather, Anholt espouses the primacy of policy and innovative action. In his view, a strategy for improving a country's reputation must be executed through substantive new economic, legal, political, social, cultural and educational activity, highlighted from time-to-time by symbolic actions that capture the imagination of publics overseas and embody the change in image that the country is seeking to make. Any global communications strategy will need to be accompanied by consistent government action over decades if it is to result in a reappraisal of the historic image.

What Brand Ireland can teach others

Ireland has leveraged its brand image to great success and, in doing so, it has shown how nation branding can be powerfully delivered without the need for a centrally managed national narrative.

Ireland has demonstrated the power of a sector-led approach in which the tourism, food and inward investment sectors pursue their own, well-researched branding strategies independently. It has demonstrated the power of expert and empowered agencies leading well-targeted brand management and communication in their own domains.

It has demonstrated the power of brand narratives that are authentically grounded in truisms of the place and its people. And it highlights the power of consistently and persistently communicating these brand elements over long periods of time, while being sufficiently flexible to reflect material change in the economic or social environment.

Most of all, it demonstrates the power of having a long-established positive country image that overseas audiences can relate to, as well as the challenge of changing aspects of such a deeply embedded image.

Notes

1 Mark Henry is the Central Marketing Director for Tourism Ireland, where he has responsibility for brand strategy, consumer insight, and communications development. Thanks to Una Fitzgibbon, Director of Marketing and Communications

at Bord Bia, and Caitriona O'Kennedy, Head of Marketing Communications at IDA Ireland, for their kind assistance.

2 For example, see the 2008 results at https://nation-branding.info/2008/10/01/ anholts-nation-brand-index-2008-released/, accessed July 2020.

3 FutureBrand (2015), 'Country Brand Index 2014–15', accessible online at www.futurebrand.com/uploads/Country-Brand-Index-2014-15.pdf, accessed July 2020.

4 Brand Finance (2019), 'Nation Brands 2019', accessible online at https://brand-finance.com/images/upload/brand_finance_nation_brands_2019_preview.pdf, accessed July 2020.

5 See the latest rankings at www.goodcountry.org/index/results/, accessed July 2020.

6 U.S. Census Bureau (2020), 'Irish-American Heritage Month and St. Patrick's Day: March 2020', www.census.gov/newsroom/facts-for-features/2020/irish-american-heritage.html, accessed July 2020.

7 Owen Bowcott (2006), 'More Britons applying for Irish passports', The Guardian online, www.theguardian.com/uk/2006/sep/13/britishidentity.travelnews, accessed July 2020.

8 Figures cited in 'Irish Diaspora' article on Wikipedia.org, https://en.wikipedia.org/wiki/Irish_diaspora, accessed July 2020.

9 'Irish Economic Performance within the EU', Ask About Ireland, www.askaboutireland.ie/reading-room/life-society/ireland-and-the-eu/irish-economic-performanc/, accessed July 2020.

10 Fanning, John (2011). 'Branding and Begorrah: The Importance of Ireland's Nation Brand Image', Irish Marketing Review, 21 (1&2), pages 23–31.

11 Foster, R. (1997), W.B. Yeats: A Life Part I, Oxford University Press, Oxford, p. 162.

12 Contained in a custom analysis of the Anholt-GfK Roper Nation Brands Index 2011 prepared for Tourism Ireland (unpublished).

13 OECD (2019), 'Statistical Insights: men's employment more dependent on trade than women's', www.oecd.org/sdd/its/statistical-insights-mens-employ-ment-more-dependent-on-trade-than-womens.htm, accessed July 2020.

14 It is placed 16th in the analysis published by Paul Joseph (2018), 'The Most and Least Visited Countries per Capita in the World' at www.travelmag.com/articles/most-and-least-visited-countries-in-the-world/, accessed July 2020.

15 Bord Bia (2020), Export Performance and Prospects 2019–2020, available online at www.bordbiaperformanceandprospects.com/annual-reports, and Sustainable Food Systems Ireland at www.sfsi.ie/agriculture-food-ireland/, accessed July 2020.

16 IBM Institute for Business Value (2019), 'Global Location Trends', online at www.ibm.com/thought-leadership/institute-business-value/report/gltr2019, accessed July 2020.

17 Clancy, Michael. (2011). 'Re-presenting Ireland: Tourism, branding and national identity in Ireland'. Journal of International Relations and Development. 14.281–308.10.1057/jird.2010.4.

18 Tourism Ireland brand guidelines (2019), www.tourismireland.com/TourismIreland/media/Tourism-Ireland/Research/Tourism-Ireland-brand-guidelines-2019.pdf, accessed August 2020.

19 Tourism Ireland's annual reports can be found at www.tourismireland.com/About-Us/Corporate-Publications/Annual-Report, accessed July 2020.

20 World Economic Forum (2019), 'The Travel & Tourism Competitiveness Report 2019', www.weforum.org/reports/the-travel-tourism-competitiveness-report-2019, accessed July 2020.

21 The initial brand concept was articulated in Bord Bia's 'Pathways for Growth' document, available at www.bordbia.ie/industry/news/press-releases/bord-bia-publishes-pathways-for-growth-for-irelands-food-sector/, accessed July 2020.

22 Una FitzGibbon (2011), 'Food Brand Ireland', https://nanopdf.com/download/food-brand-ireland-una-fitzgibbon-august-30-2011_pdf, accessed July 2020.

23 More details at www.origingreen.ie/, accessed July 2020.

24 Fanning, John (2006) The Importance of Being Branded: An Irish Perspective, Dublin: The Liffey Press.

25 The full list is available at https://en.wikipedia.org/wiki/List_of_diplomatic_missions_of_Ireland, accessed July 2020.

26 Seth Linder (2019), 'Ireland's Greening of the World', Dublin: O'Brien Press.

27 These are the Wild Atlantic Way (encompassing the west coast), the Hidden Heartlands, Ireland's Ancient East, and Dublin – Surprising by Nature. More information on these can be found on the website of the National Tourism Development Agency, Fáilte Ireland, at www.failteireland.ie/.

28 John Fanning and Mark Henry (2012), 'Brand Ireland should be rethought and replaced', The Irish Times, 27 July 2012, available online at www.irishtimes.com/opinion/brand-ireland-should-be-rethought-and-replaced-1.543783, accessed July 2020.

29 See the Central Statistics Office of Ireland's 'Statistical Yearbook of Ireland' series at www.cso.ie/en/statistics/statisticalyearbookofireland/, accessed July 2020.

30 Accessible online at https://merrionstreet.ie/MerrionStreet/en/ImageLibrary/20180622_Global_Ireland.pdf, accessed July 2020.

31 Simon Anholt (2010), 'Places: Identity, Image and Reputation', Palgrave Macmillan, page 5.

12 Portugal

João Freire

Introduction

Developing a brand strategy involves setting objectives and channelling resources to better serve certain target markets. The same logic applies to nation branding, but the complexity is far greater and requires some adaptations. One of the complexities is that the responsibility to brand a nation often lies with a central government that makes policy-based decisions built into its political manifesto. This implies difficulties in having a long-term view for the brand since in democratic countries one expects governments to change every few years.

Another complex aspect is the identification and involvement of different target markets in the process. Target markets include both internal and external stakeholders. Internal stakeholders exist within a country and include citizens, local government, companies and other organizations. External stakeholders exist outside of a country and can be broadly identified by three types of target markets: tourists, labour and investors. Internal and external stakeholders are essential to the development of a successful nation brand strategy, but these different stakeholders are made up of a large set of distinct individuals and organizations with different needs.

The UN World Tourism Organization's (UNWTO's) definition of tourists is an example of the extent of these stakeholders. Tourists include those travelling for pleasure as well as people doing business or people looking for healthcare. Therefore, branding a nation is a complicated endeavour. Some countries handle the complexity by assigning different aspects of the nation brand to distinctive organizations.

In the case of Portugal, responsibility for the management of the Portugal brand is currently shared by two different organizations, Tourism of Portugal and Portugal Global – Trade & Investment Agency (AICEP). Both organizations are under the auspices of the Ministry of Economy, but they operate independently from one another and in an isolated way. Tourism of

DOI: 10.4324/9781003084051-12

Portugal focuses on tourism and has its strategy for brand Portugal. AICEP focuses on the attraction of investment and internationalization of Portuguese companies. It has its own strategy for brand Portugal. Because these two organizations focus on different markets, operate independently and have their own strategies, Portugal can be said to be one country served by two brands.

Tourism of Portugal

Tourism of Portugal manages the tourism industry in Portugal and owns the exclusive license of the brand Visit Portugal. Its logo was created in 1992 by well-known Portuguese artist, José de Guimarães. The logo contains the colours of the Portuguese flag, a sun symbolizing the warmth of the local people and ocean waves symbolizing the historical maritime expansion of Portugal. A simpler interpretation of the Visit Portugal logo could be 'sun and sea'. This logo is used exclusively by Tourism of Portugal within the tourism industry.

Tourism of Portugal acts in four distinct areas: promotion of tourism in Portugal and abroad; to support companies within the tourism industry; to qualify and train human resources; and to regulate and inspect casinos.

Tourism of Portugal's key responsibility is to create the conditions in Portugal to have a competitive offer within the tourism industry. It achieves this by regulating the industry and guaranteeing a level of quality, as well as through financing companies and specific activities that are aligned with the designed strategy for the industry. Tourism of Portugal is also responsible for the technical schools that exist to train people to work in the tourism industry. The scope of Tourism of Portugal is vast and the organization truly manages the tourism industry in Portugal.

In order to be more inclusive and ensure a reach to local organizations and companies in the different areas of Portugal, Tourism of Portugal has divided the country into seven individual regional tourism destinations. Five regions are located on mainland Portugal: Porto and North of Portugal, Centre, Lisbon, Alentejo and the Algarve. The two archipelagos, Azores and Madeira, are autonomous regions of Portugal and operate with more independence than the mainland Portugal regions.

Each individual destination manages all aspects of its local operations and has a budget to promote its region within Portugal. Nonetheless, to obtain financial support for promotion in international markets each region must follow guidelines set by Tourism of Portugal.

The guidelines are usually linked with the promotion of specific tourism products to pre-established international destinations as defined in Tourism of Portugal's strategic plan. The aim is to create a coherent strategy for the promotion of Portugal in international markets. It is a robust model with clear objectives and guidelines. Nevertheless, it may be argued that the strategy defined is focused on selling tourism products rather than on developing a brand strategy. In fact, Tourism of Portugal's branding strategy for Portugal is not clear.

By examining the vision defined by Tourism of Portugal, it may be concluded that one objective for the Portugal brand is to become a sustainable tourist destination:

Affirm tourism as a hub for economic, social and environmental development throughout the territory, positioning Portugal as one of the most competitive and sustainable tourist destinations in the world.[1] (*Tourism of Portugal*).

Although sustainability is a declared objective of Tourism of Portugal, there is no clear strategy for its implementation at the regional or national level. The vision does not translate into actions on the part of regional destinations except for the Azores, which is clearly positioned as a sustainable tourist destination. The Azores is the only destination with an organization managing the implementation of all elements related to sustainability in order to achieve the positioning.

The strategic plan currently defined for the Portugal brand by Tourism of Portugal is based on ten strategic assets: people, climate and light, history and culture, sea, nature, water, gastronomy and wines, cultural arts, sport and business events, well-being and living in Portugal. However, it is not clear how these assets translate into a clear value proposition and brand positioning for Portugal. It is also unclear what is the value proposition of Portugal.

Even with the lack of a clear value proposition, tourism in Portugal has been quite successful the past few years. It has seen the number of arrivals increase by double digits, a massive investment in infrastructure and a substantial increase in both the supply of hotels and the number of short-term rental properties. Portugal has also been awarded multiple tourism industry awards.

Nevertheless, the rapid expansion of tourism has had an adverse impact on some regions of Portugal. The increasingly expensive housing prices in Lisbon have affected the local people and many traditional neighbourhoods are now unaffordable. These neighbourhoods have seen a substantial decrease in local population and a substantial increase in tourists.

Cities, especially Lisbon and Porto, are clearly suffering from overtourism and tourismphobia. This can be observed from many perspectives:

tourists, tourism industry, local people, local and central governmental organizations. One can argue that in general the two big winners of mass tourism – from where overtourism and tourismophobia originate – are the tourism industry with its increased revenues and the government, both local and central, with its increased tax revenues.

One potential loser from mass tourism is local people who are not dependent on the tourism industry to make a living. With increased tourism, these stakeholders may be unable to afford to live in their own city, enjoy local amenities or other spaces that were previously available to them. The tourist is another potential loser since a part of his/her experience, the authenticity of a place, could disappear. If local people and local elements start to disappear, then the appeal of a place for the tourist who is actively looking for local character and who values a local experience will also be reduced. Other industries could also potentially be negatively affected by overtourism. For example, it might be harder to attract certain companies or students to a place if office space or housing prices become too expensive or completely unavailable.

The increase in tourism – now occupying space and absorbing local labour – may also negatively affect flourishing industries. In this sense, what a place gains with tourism it may be losing in other industries. The economic balance of a place might be lost, which could ultimately threaten the competitiveness of the place.

The previously described circumstances have been seen in Portugal and are the effect of the lack of a coherent national strategy for the Portugal brand. While there is a strategic plan in place for the development of the Portuguese tourism industry, there is no brand management. One cannot identify a clear value proposition and positioning nor a model of managing and controlling the tourism industry in a way that safeguards local people and reduces the impact of tourism on other industries.

For these reasons, there is a need to reorganize and manage tourism in a more integrated way with the rest of the market. To accomplish this, it would be important to involve other organizations, such as the Portuguese Trade Office – AICEP, in the management of the Portugal brand and to ensure that all relevant internal and external stakeholders are engaged.

AICEP

AICEP is a governmental organization operating under the Ministry of Economy with a clear set of goals and objectives. The purpose of AICEP is to attract investment and to support Portuguese companies in their internationalization. It is organized by key accounts that manage potential investment projects. The nature of the operation of AICEP is typically B2B:

> *Aicep Portugal Global – Trade & Investment Agency (AICEP) is a government business entity, focused on encouraging the best foreign companies to invest in Portugal and contribute to the success of Portuguese companies abroad in their internationalization processes or export activities.*[2]

AICEP focuses on creating a positive image of Portugal to help exports and to increase the attractiveness of Portugal as a place to invest. This implies that AICEP is also mandated to manage the Portugal brand, which involves defining a value proposition.

AICEP's value proposition for Portugal is strongly based on the business environment in Portugal, strategic location, access to key markets, availability of skilled human resources, lower costs and good infrastructures. Moreover, another important element in AICEP's value proposition is a certain lifestyle that can be enjoyed in Portugal:

> *Furthermore, Portugal is not only a good country to invest but also a most desirable place to live. A place to visit and enjoy. You can find here a safe, environmentally responsible, with privileged nature, rich leisure and culture and with high quality healthcare facilities. Portugal is blessed by abundant sunlight and warm temperatures that, certainly, makes you feel motivated and productive.*[3]

AICEP has a considerably lower budget than Tourism of Portugal and they lack the resources to advertise internationally. Consequently, the bulk of Portugal's international promotion comes from Tourism of Portugal.

Adding to the complexity of managing the Portugal brand, AICEP is not the only Portuguese organization with a mandate to attract investment and promote Portuguese exports. In 2009 Portugal started a process of creating clusters comprised of companies, universities and other organizations involved in research and development (R&D). The Portuguese government granted financial support to small and medium sized companies and aggregated organizations into specific clusters to develop high-value projects. The formation of clusters created a dynamic process that currently consists of 18 clusters operating in different industries and areas of the Portuguese economy, including fashion, aeronautical, health, tourism, and so on. The mission statement for the 18 clusters states that the major motivation of the clusters is to promote exports. This implies that each cluster is responsible for attracting international investors to its specific area and promoting its members in the international market.

Initially, the aim was to create a single brand to represent the 18 clusters with a cohesive communication message. The differentiation among clusters was to be done by identifying the specific area where the cluster operated. Nonetheless when the branding project was finalized some of the clusters were already operational and these clusters did not accept the idea of a single unified brand. Each cluster then created its own brand with its own communication budget and structure. The ramification of this was a diminishing awareness of each cluster and the loss of economies of scale and synergies. Instead of having one team with an allocated budget for all 18 clusters, they now have 18 individual teams and budgets. To this day, there continues to be 18 different cluster entities promoting the Portugal brand in international markets.

The 18 clusters are supervised by the Institute to Support Small and Medium Sized Companies (IAPMEI), a Portuguese governmental organization. Theoretically IAPMEI should have the job of coordinating the communication of the clusters. In practice there is little evidence that this is done. Moreover, after reviewing the management structures of AICEP and IAPMEI, it is clear that there is little direct or functional connection between the two organizations. In other words, the Portugal brand with regard to the areas of attraction of investment and promotion of exports is being managed by both AICEP *and* the 18 clusters, with little or no coordination between them.

Therefore, in reality Portugal is not one country with two brands but one country with 20 brands. Tourism of Portugal manages the Portugal brand for tourism while AICEP and the 18 clusters manage the Portugal brand for foreign direct investment (FDI) and the promotion of exports.

Conclusion

It cannot be said that there is a cohesive brand strategy for Portugal. There are strategies in place for different industries, of which tourism is the most successful. Tourism of Portugal has done a superb job in the promotion of the destination and the transformation of the industry. Portugal has been named the Best Tourist Destination in Europe at the World Travel Awards (WTA) 4 years in a row (2017–2020). Nonetheless, on the attraction of FDI Portugal still lags behind. In 2019, EY ranked Portugal 17th on the European FDI destination countries.

The success story of tourism in the past decade can be traced to a strong organization based on regional destinations with good integration of different stakeholders. Tourism of Portugal has a significant promotional budget indicating that awareness of the need to build brand Portugal has increased for tourism, but less so for FDI. A less successful FDI story emphasizes the lack of a coherent strategy and too many organizations with limited capability currently promoting the Portugal brand. The lack of a unified brand diminishes the power of lobbying for legislation that would increase the competitiveness of Portugal. Therefore, it would be appropriate to move towards a single organization managing all aspects of the Portugal brand.

Another consequence of not having a single organizational structure managing the brand is the possibility of having untapped or unexplored segments. A clear example of a segment that is not being managed is international students. None of the organizations prioritize this segment and there are no mechanisms in place to manage it. The Ministry of Education could be responsible for coordinating this segment, but activity in this domain has been limited. This can be seen in the complex guidelines for international students.

All of this highlights that there is currently no clear strategy for the Portugal brand. There are many organizations working with the Portugal brand with little to no coordination between them. As it stands, Portugal's value proposition is unclear and not well defined. There are few economies of scale in the promotion of Portugal or synergies between the different industries.

Reflection on a lost opportunity

In 2007, attempts were made to develop a branding strategy that could integrate all aspects of the Portuguese economy into a well-defined value proposition. AICEP and Tourism of Portugal launched a campaign created by Pedro Bidarra of BBDO called 'Portugal, Europe's West Coast'. The idea was to create a parallel between Portugal and California, USA. California, on America's west coast, is known for both its innovation and lifestyle. This could have been the basis of a branding effort for Portugal. But this ended up being an advertising campaign or a propaganda tool of the government of the day. The project did not mature and did not involve the society at large. If it had involved all levels of society such as local government, central government, companies and investors it could have been a serious branding exercise.

The branding effort would have required a central structure with the full support of the central government as well as the main opposition parties. Creating this type of structure and commitment would have prepared the stable environment necessary for the development of a long-term brand strategy consisting of one structure with an executive board overseeing the different economic areas and coordinating its efforts. If this had been done, it would have taken into account all stakeholders and there would have been a better management of all industries.

Notes

1 https://travelbi.turismodeportugal.pt/en-US/pages/sustentabilidade.aspx
2 www.portugalglobal.pt/EN/about-us/Pages/about-us.aspx
3 www.portugalglobal.pt/EN/Portugal/Pages/WelcometoPortugal.aspx

13 Estonia

José Filipe Torres

Origins and structure

The nation brand builders responsible for Estonia's current perceptions fall under the umbrella of Enterprise Estonia (EAS), an organization whose structure was built from scratch with a now all-encompassing role which originated from three principle areas of activity; developing Estonian enterprises and boosting export capacity, increasing tourism revenue, and bringing high value-added foreign investments to Estonia (Enterprise Estonia). Enterprise Estonia was created as *the* institution who would prepare Estonia nation brand's strategic objectives in terms of providing financing and training to encourage entrepreneurship. EAS is headed by a two-member Management Board and a Supervisory Board made up of entrepreneurs and officials, supported by various advisory boards consisting of area experts on behalf of Enterprise Estonia who give the organization advice and guidance in return for strategic, relevant information (Enterprise Estonia). Designated a public sector organization, Enterprise Estonia implements policies on behalf of the Ministry of Economic Affairs and Communications.

The nation brand objective presented by Enterprise Estonia aims to contribute to its overall Global Competitiveness ranking through the promotion of innovation and the development of entrepreneurial business models. Enterprise Estonia's commitment to its three dimensions; increasing exports, attracting foreign investment, and increasing tourism allow for clear key performance indicators (KPIs) in terms of objective setting and benchmark analysis. This process directly impacts their strategy's success. Enterprise Estonia uses specific nation brand tools that ensure key indicators and measure the relevance of the strategy in terms of meeting specific goals.

The unique structure of Enterprise Estonia as a nation brand management organization is that it is made up of stakeholders and nation brand builders alike, overseeing both definitive nation branding activities as well

DOI: 10.4324/9781003084051-13

as nation marketing and promotional efforts being performed directly by the respective stakeholder organization. The aforementioned three primary areas of activity have driven the enterprise's mission since 2000, when it was established in terms of economic development, leading to the creation and oversight of the Estonian Investment Agency (EIA) and Estonia Tourist Board as well as since expanding its services to include the promotion and facilitation of relocation to Estonia (Work in Estonia), the B2B platform offering Estonia nation brand management communication and storytelling tools and information (Brand Estonia) to reaffirm their very real and consistently validated essence and *Central Idea*.

Two additional fundamental services that Enterprise Estonia collaboratively oversees are the e-Residency programme and the e-Estonia Briefing Centre. Estonia was the first country to offer an e-Residency programme, a government-issued digital identity and status which provides access to Estonia's e-services and transparent business environment (e-Residency). E-Estonia Briefing Centre is an executive centre and innovation hub based in Tallin, specially designed to experience the e-state of mind. Established in 2009 as an NGO, today it finds itself a part of Enterprise Estonia and has an integral role in e-Estonia brand and country promotion (e-Estonia).

Brand Estonia and its dimensions

With a clear vision of the future as a digital society, Estonia invested heavily in digital infrastructure, becoming the first e-State. They did so by creating digital infrastructure and e-solutions to make life easier for both their citizens and companies. This meant that 99% of public services are now digitally managed and accessible online, cutting the red tape in state processes.

Estonia was already being perceived as a digital society and was thus incorporated into the brand strategy. Having acted accordingly, Estonia has been successful in curating a nation brand and aligning perceptions with reality by incorporating digitally focused activations and resources across all aspects of the nation brand offering. This case will further explore the various dimensions of the Estonian nation brand in greater detail, but the key component as to why they have each been successful derives from their consistent validation of the *Central Idea*. This *Central Idea* provides the foundation for a coherent, consistent and realistic strategy capable of structuring the entire brand. The majority of actions, activities, measures, and policies are aligned with this concept, making it possible to enhance perceptions and manage their reputation.

Brand Estonia is the primary method of brand communication to domestic professional stakeholders, which offers extensive information on the nation brand purpose and method of delivery. The *story* of Brand Estonia

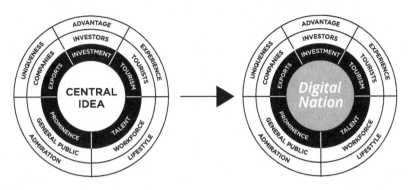

Figure 13.1 Estonian Nation Brand *Central Idea*
Source: Bloom Consulting Nation Brand Wheel©

provides authorities with core messages which directly relate to the *Central Idea* of the brand; digital society, independent minds, and clean environment. Brand Estonia has gone above and beyond to be the instigator as well as the actor by creating and gathering extensive content (toolbox; photos, videos, presentations, prints, graphics, typefaces, audio) for the benefit of a range of stakeholders who wish to positively and accurately represent themselves through the use of Brand Estonia.

In my view, Brand Estonia has similarly made efforts to brand itself amidst a greater region of nearby countries as a point of leverage for its own nation brand. Estonia has taken the course of disassociating itself from the Baltic countries and rather shifted its efforts towards being recognized as one of the Nordic countries due to its overwhelmingly positive connotation established over many years. Brand Estonia would prefer to be associated with the Nordic's in the scope of *pragmatic, honest, straightforward, egalitarian,* and *close to nature* with the effect of enhancing perceptions of Estonia as a trustworthy nation (Brand Estonia).

Estonia was able to identify an extremely important factor given its influence and the impact that it can have on the remaining components of a nation brand, the concept of Digital Identity.

They have demonstrated their comprehensive understanding that the offline and online world are intrinsically linked and influence one another. Estonia has become a benchmark country for those who promote and act on their Digital Identity by investing in their online presence early on. In searching for "*Estonia*" on various search engines, everything that appears is a reflection of its *Central Idea*. The digital perception of the nation reflects its intended one, and the same perception, more importantly, corresponds with reality.

Before further elaborating on the primary areas of focus, the **Bloom Consulting Nation Brand Wheel©** will help to define the strategic nation branding progression of Estonia. Each measurable in their own regard in terms of attraction and appeal and influenced by the nation brand, the five dimensions which make up the wheel are investment, tourism, talent, prominence, and exports. Each dimension caters to a specific target audience; investors, tourists, workforce, general public, and companies (respectively). Nation branding strategies are furthermore implemented to work on their behalf with consideration for the unique needs of each target audience; advantages, experience, lifestyle, admiration, and uniqueness (respectively).

Enterprise Estonia's focus within the dimension of **exports**, in cooperation with Trade with Estonia, is to develop more complex products and services and helping enterprises to enter foreign markets while improving market and business analysis capabilities (Enterprise Estonia). Export diversification and expansion of business opportunities through building a greater basis of data made available to clients is an example of brand behaviour, and act which validates the nation's *Central Idea*. Enterprise Estonia's actions reflect, each to some level, its outset mission of being a digital society and furthermore one of independent minds, primarily one that provides *easy and straightforward communication with the state* (Brand Estonia).

Within the dimension of **foreign investment**, EAS is driven to diversify the Estonian economy. Responsible for promoting foreign investments in Estonia and assessing international companies in finding business opportunities, The Estonian Investment Agency (EIA), is a government agency which sits under the umbrella of Enterprise Estonia (Invest in Estonia). Returning to the point that EAS is a uniquely designed organization as it would be standard practice for the nation brand builders to meet the sole objective of increasing the appeal and attraction for investment rather than simultaneously promoting and facilitating it.

Enterprise Estonia's cross competences of perceptions and placemaking necessitate mutually beneficial information sharing with policymakers regarding their efforts within the economic environment, working towards solutions to eliminate bottlenecks for the purpose of increasing international competitiveness (Enterprise Estonia). Enterprise Estonia seeks to earn a stronger reputation for ease of doing through practical legislation as it will only ameliorate investor attractiveness and provide support to pre-existing investors in terms of business development. With the outset goal of bringing in 1.5 billion euros worth of foreign investment within 5 years, and benefit from the creation of 5,000 high value-added jobs (Enterprise Estonia),

EAS is walking the walk of increased investor appeal and attraction through the implementation of activities which speak to the *Central Idea* of Brand Estonia.

Enterprise Estonia seeks to increase the revenue generated by the dimension of **tourism** through supporting innovative and distinctive tourism products and services (Enterprise Estonia). The primary objective is to capture the attention of potential visitors through unspoken character; Nordic, surprising, and smart, each carry with it an effect that aims to convey the essence of Estonia. EAS hopes to secure desire to travel to Estonia while focusing on capacity building for high tourism revenue per capita fields such as business, conference, and smart services (Enterprise Estonia). To maximize competitiveness, the necessary investments must first be made to penetrate certain market segments and increase attractiveness via feasibility and accessibility with the goal of increasing the export of tourism services to 2.6 billion euros over 5 years and increase the number of international conferences to 100 (Enterprise Estonia). In terms of penetrating new leisure markets, Estonia has placed a focus on Chinese travellers who are actively visiting nearby nations such as Finland who receive 10 times as many overnight stays of Chinese tourists when compared to Estonia (Enterprise Estonia). Enterprise Estonia has laid out the many partnerships with which they will work to increase the number of Asian tourists including the European Travel Commission and airlines such as Finnair to establish a greater level of air connectivity (Enterprise Estonia). That said, Estonia's tourism industry is equally as dependent on ameliorating international perceptions to drum up tourist Interest as is the investment in infrastructure, hence why consistent brand validation and cross communication between place makers and nation brand builders is vital.

Enterprise Estonia maintains consideration for three key topics during the implementation and execution of dimensional activities; Estonia's reputation abroad, the innovation readiness and courage of enterprises, and making the right choices when distributing the limited resources of a small country, demanding the availability of high-quality information and the ability to analyse it within the industries and at the level of the value chains of industries. (Enterprise Estonia).

The monetary goal of Enterprise Estonia is seen through by their respective organization, the Estonian Tourist Board, while goals of attractiveness and appeal hold accountable Brand Estonia and Visit Estonia as it demands consistent storytelling, communication, and specific brand behaviour which can be gauged via proof points and competitiveness across the dimensions.

Enterprise Estonia is responsible for establishing Work in Estonia, one of the operational drivers that is supported by the nation brand's attraction and appeal for the **talent** dimension. Acting as a digital source of information with a comprehensive directory for vacant positions available to the domestic and international community, Work in Estonia offers a breadth of services in terms of job support, visas and residence, and everyday life (Work in Estonia). Beyond Work in Estonia, additional resources have been created such as Study in Estonia and Research in Estonia. Although they live outside of the EAS umbrella, these resources work in tandem to attract and appeal to those seeking international experience and the possibility of relocation to a country whose *Central Idea* resonates with them. One of the most well-known and globally discussed initiatives already mentioned, the e-Residency programme, proved successful enough to be reimagined in other countries.

Proof that it works

Consistent implementation of the *Central Idea* of Estonia nation brand has resulted in changing and building the right reputation among internal and external audiences. This is evident in Estonia's performance in various international rankings.

According to the 2019 edition of the European Commission's Digital Economy and Society Index (DESI), which monitors progress made by EU countries in terms of digitalization, Estonia ranks 8th among the 28 Member States. It is one of the European leaders when it comes to digital public services. In addition, it is the best rated country in the 2018 Digital Life Abroad, given the availability of online administrative and government services. It also ranks highly on the 2020 Internet Freedom House Index. Estonia's success in ranking in terms of a digital lifestyle is assumedly a great deal thanks to its implementation and development of the e-Residency programme which has turned Estonia into the ideal place for digital nomads and international entrepreneurs planning to start an EU-based company.

Often ranked as one of the most competitive, open, and transparent economies in the world (ranked 8th in the 2021 Heritage Foundation's Index of Economic Freedom), its simple and agile business environment is one of its main drivers.

A further indicator that Estonia nation brand strategy has been a success, and that all of the policies adopted along with it are having a real impact on public perception, is the result in digital searches.

As a performance metric for nation and place brands, online searches show how a country, region or city is doing in terms of appeal and attraction and how much proactive interest is generated in the desired international audiences. The more a country, region or city is searched for the right reasons, the more interesting it is for its audience. Online searches are a true indicator of how a place is perceived by international stakeholders. What people search about a place is what they associate with it. In other words, if a country region or city is digitally searched with positive keywords, it has a strong and relevant brand.

To assess and analyse the digital performance of Estonia, we used the Digital Demand – D2© software. This intelligence tool allows us to understand the appeal of nation and place brands, while providing us with an overview of the most searched topics (or brandtags) in the five dimensions of the **Bloom Consulting Nation Brand Wheel©**.

In recent years, Estonia has become the fasted growing country in Europe for searches related to "Entrepreneurship", a brandtag clearly linked to Estonia's *Central Idea*. With an average growth of 83% in Digital Demand – D2©, Estonia's growth is ten times higher than the world's average growth (8.7%).

Estonia is also one of the fastest growing European countries in terms of attracting talent, another topic directly associated with the *Central Idea*. Having implemented programmes such as e-Residency and other policies that align with the country's *Central Idea*. Estonia is the country brand with the third largest growth rate in terms of "Work" brandtag searches in Europe according to the Digital Demand – D2© software. The strategy has

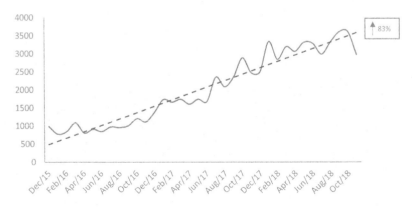

Figure 13.2 Global Searches for Estonia

Evolution of searches concerning the Brandtag "Entrepreneurship" (December 2015 – October 2018)

Source: Bloom Consulting and D2 – Analytics ©

Table 13.1 World Ranking for "Entrepreneurship" search themes

Rank	Country
1	Canada
2	China
3	Singapore
4	India
5	Japan
6	Israel
7	Estonia
8	Hong Kong
9	Chile
10	United Kingdom

Ranking of searches for the "Entrepreneurship" Brandtag (Global searches 2018)

Source: Bloom Consulting and D2 – Analytics ©

succeeded in aligning the *Central Idea* and reality of the country brand with international perceptions.

Estonia is not only the number one in Europe for average growth in entrepreneurship searches, but number seven in the world. The country is ahead of others like Hong Kong, Chile, and the United Kingdom.

Going beyond a digital society

Looking towards the future of Brand Estonia, it would appear the nation brand builders at the helm are moving beyond a *digital society* as the sole pillar of attractiveness. The core messages being conveyed by stakeholders, professionals and citizens across the nation maintain the importance of digital society but include and equally focus on *independent minds* and *clean environment* as was noted previously. Estonia's list of "firsts" within the digital world is impressive, and they know that. However, Enterprise Estonia is also aware that the world commends them for their accomplishments, and it is the perfect opportunity to use the momentum gained from digital success stories and use it as a platform to elevate their other accomplishments, goals and values.

Sources

Enterprise Estonia. (2021) www.eas.ee/wp-content/uploads/2019/06/EAS_Strategiline_Kava_190614_ENG.pdf, assessed on September 8, 2020.

Freedom House. (2021) https://freedomhouse.org/countries/freedom-net/scores, assessed on March 23, 2021.

Index of Economic Freedom. (2021) www.heritage.org/index/country/estonia, assessed on March 23, 2021.

Index